Xcelerate

the evangelist's heartbeat

by_Matt Wilson
and _Andy Hawthorne

Scripture Union, 207–209 Queensway, Bletchley, MK2 2EB, England.
www.scriptureunion.org.uk

Scripture Union is an international Christian charity working with churches in more than 130 countries providing resources to bring the good news about Jesus Christ to children, young people and families – and to encourage them to develop spiritually through the Bible and prayer.

As well as our network of volunteers, staff and associates who run holidays, church-based events and school Christian groups, we produce a wide range of publications and support those who use our resources through training programmes.

ISBN 1 85999 607 8

British Library Cataloguing-in-Publication Data
A catalogue record for this book is available from the British Library.

Book Cover and Internal design by Martin Lore
mlore@dircon.co.uk.
Printed and bound in Great Britain by Creative Print and Design (Wales) Ebbw Vale

Contents

Foreword by Luis Palau

For years I have admired the ministry of The Message Trust from a distance, seeing its great impact. Then the first time I met Matt and Andy it became immediately clear that – even though we are based on opposite sides of the globe – we share a passion. Round that breakfast table there was no need for lengthy introductions. It was obvious that here were two men whose driving force was the desire to win lost young people, men and women for the kingdom of God.

The message of the gospel of Jesus Christ, stated so clearly in John 3:16 and 1 Corinthians 15:3–5, is sacred and unchanging, but the methods of proclaiming the message are not. The apostle Paul willingly and actively proclaimed the gospel using every available method. He could say, 'I have become all things to all men so that by all possible means I might save some' (1 Corinthians 9:22). Any method is valid as long as it is ethical and moral. There are no biblical restraints on methodology, only on the message.

Indeed, it was a dramatic shift in evangelistic method – from the traditional stadium 'crusade' or 'mission' popularised by Billy Graham to our new 'festival' model of outreach – and the amazing testimony of Message 2000 that brought Andy, Matt and me together that morning in Manchester. They represent to me the energy and creativity of the new generation with their constantly evolving strategies and initiatives to impact Greater Manchester with the claims of Jesus Christ. We knew that our two ministries could work together with great effect to extend the kingdom of God in that city. What I've observed from a distance I'm now tasting! I think that what the Lord has begun here can transform the city of Manchester and become a model for other cities.

Evangelism, especially on this city-wide scale, is nothing short of spiritual warfare. The enemy doesn't want his territory invaded or those he has held captive being released. In warfare good intelligence is a battle-winner. Knowing our own strengths and weaknesses, as well as those of the spiritual enemy, Satan, is vitally important, and there is much in this book that will equip and strengthen you as you seek to be used by God to reach out to save those who are perishing. We live in a special time, as in the days of John Wesley when England was in worse shape than the inner city is today. I'm sure that God has raised up Matt and Andy for the task of building His kingdom in this great nation.

Andy and Matt are the new generation, but they have the same evangelist's heartbeat that Paul expressed in his letter to the believers in 1 Corinthians 9:16, 'Woe to me if I do not preach the gospel!' He seems to be describing a physical pain in his soul, experienced if he does not preach the good news. That same passion and determination – that fire – is the hallmark of these two men.

Only touch this book if you don't mind getting scorched!

Luis Palau is a world-renowned evangelist –
you can check out his website at www.palau.org.

introduction

The Heart of the Evangelist
by Andy Hawthorne

An evangelist needs the head of a father,
the heart of a mother and the skin of a rhinoceros.
Spurgeon

Upside Down Mission

Message 2000, the massive youth mission held in the millennium summer right here in Manchester, was the biggest faith adventure to date for the boys and girls at *The Message Trust*. In the build-up to it, there were days when I seriously wished I had never met the bearded wonder, Mike Pilavachi, and he probably felt the same way about me. A couple of years earlier, over a luke-warm cup of coffee at *Spring Harvest*, we'd come up with the crazy idea of cancelling *Soul Survivor*, the biggest youth festival in Europe and shipping the thousands of young people wholesale to Manchester for mission instead. It's true to say that the sheer logistics and finances of the enterprise stretched both our ministries to the limit but we wouldn't have missed it for the world. We saw God do some wonderful things right across the city and amazingly enough, we even came out of it the best of mates – and are daft enough to be well on our way with plans to do it all again but even bigger!!!

The lessons we learnt were numerous but one of the key ones was this: THE GOSPEL WORKS in any and every situation, no matter how dark, it was kind of re-revelation. When you can actually feel the spiritual atmosphere of whole geographic areas change, as a result of young people preaching the gospel in word and deed, it gives you a new confidence in the Christian message. A new desire to spread it everywhere starts burning. I'm absolutely convinced that the problem we have in this nation is not with the gospel; the problem is simply that it's not out there. We're keeping it to ourselves or, at best, only spreading it about liberally in certain 'nice' areas when the whole nation in every nook and cranny needs a mighty dose of the good news of Jesus.

The other thing that came home to us big time in 2000 is that the day of the superstar evangelist is over. I'm all for anointing, and some men and women clearly have powerful evangelistic ministries, but what happened at *Message 2000* was a total eye-opener. Rather than one big evangelist walking into town and thousands of spectators watching him expectantly, we had no Big Names but 11,000 anonymous evangelists out there doing the business – not on a stage, but where it counts in the mess and grime of everyday Manchester communities. You could say that *Message 2000* turned mission on its head. The result was a far greater impact than we had ever imagined – not just on the people we were trying to reach but on the people who were doing the reaching. Nothing quite prepared us for what God did with his people as they got busy with the very business that the church is meant to be for, relevantly reaching and caring for a hurting world.

For Your Eyes Only

The financial provision was, as is so often the case, staggering and hair-raising. It really was the 11th hour and 59th minute before all the money came in. What was even more amazing was the team God called to be involved. We had the most fantastic people here in Manchester, many of them working for no pay simply because they had caught the vision of this mega-youth mission. One of these people was Matt Wilson – he'd come out of university with a first-class honours degree, was working at a local design studio and was undoubtedly on a career path that would result very soon in lots of status and a vast wad in his back pocket every month. Fortunately for us, God got hold of him and challenged him to give up two years from his career in order to work for *Message 2000* as the campaign manager, after which he could slip back into the business and resume plan A.

However, it wasn't long, before I realised God might have something better for Matt in the long term – i.e. not a lot of status, not a lot of money but loads of treasure in heaven. I started praying about how we at *The Message Trust* could use Matt after *Message 2000*. We had thought for some time that it would be good to set up a training school in Manchester to mobilise and equip young people. As I prayed, it became obvious to me that Matt could be the man to head this up, so early in 2000, I approached him with the idea of working together to set up the new training school. To be honest, Matt seemed less than impressed with the idea but being the good lad that he is, he promised to go away and pray about it. I got the distinct impression that he wasn't up for it though. About a week later, a piece of paper marked 'Private and confidential: For Your Eyes Only' arrived on my desk. I furtively looked round my office to check for any hidden cameras and then opened it. It was from Matt, who explained that God had woken him up at 3 am the previous morning and filled his mind with ideas for the school.

'It should be an Evangelists' Training School,' he said. 'That's our distinctive characteristic. Let's identify radical young evangelists from around the nation, train them in knowledge, character, skills and motivation and then send them out in the power of the Spirit all over the place to bring in the harvest.'

I love it when God does a number on people, especially when he agrees with me! Matt and I arranged to meet about a week later in Norwich, at the Pioneer Conference where we were planning to bang the drum about *Message 2000*. Matt said 'Let's pray about it, but not tell anyone just yet.' I think he was secretly hoping that God might change his mind and release him back into the ministry of earning vast wads!

'*Pioneer*' people are great but often go in for slightly unusual ministry times which involve pulling people from the audience and embarrassing them in front of lots of people. At this particular conference, it was my turn. Gerald Coates spotted me and asked me to come to the front. He then proceeded to pray over me while pouring a five-litre bottle of water over my head. If only I'd told him I was an Anglican! Then he asked a group of men to come and lift me up, as if on an altar. So there I was, high above the 4,000-strong congregation, thinking, 'I don't want to be here, and if any of these chaps touches my bottom, I might just have to smack him one', when Martin Scott, one of Gerald's co-workers, started to prophesy over me.

It went something like this: '*You haven't told anyone about this yet, but it is on your heart to set up a training school in Manchester for young believers who will come to Manchester for five or six months, to be trained and catch a vision for what you do and then be sent out all over the world to bring in the harvest. Press on with this idea because it is from the Lord and it will be very fruitful.*'

Matt was standing directly opposite me with his chin on the floor and an expression that said, '*We're in trouble now!*'

What you read between the covers of this book is not so much a systematic *Xcelerate* course syllabus but an unpacking of Matt's vision and passion. As far as I'm concerned, he's expressing the heartbeat of an increasing number of God's people. I'm even arrogant enough to think he might have caught a bit of this stuff from me, as we've worked closely together for the last few years. Matt and his team have made sure that *Xcelerate* has now well and truly screeched off the grid. The first group of students joined us in February 2001 for five months of hardcore training and equipping to reach out to this hurting generation. Subsequent intakes have established the training programme as an indispensable part of what we do. It seems to be an idea for which the time has come. I believe with my whole heart that this is the day of the evangelist – that God is starting to raise up an army of young evangelists who will work in teams and give their whole lives to presenting the gospel in word and deed, wherever they go.

The Perfect Partnership – Worship and Evangelism

For the past couple of decades, God has blessed the church through worship and we are indebted to young guys such as Matt Redman, Martin Smith and Tim Hughes for whom worship is the highest priority and who have given themselves to writing Jesus-centred songs of adoration for the church.

The more time I spent with them and the lovely worshippers at *Soul Survivor*, the more confused I became. I knew that 'man's chief end was to worship God and enjoy him forever' and all that stuff, but how does that fit in with the great commission and Jesus' burning heart for the whole world to be saved? Anyway, here's the answer I believe the Lord gave me. It's only as we worship that we get a true sense of just how awesome our God is, and how extravagant and white-hot is his love for people like us. In this context, we get to the place where we can't bear it that he isn't getting the praise he deserves from his creation and that the people he made are missing out on the ecstatic joy of being in touch with their creator. So we go out in the power of the Spirit with the avowed intention of seeing people saved and new worshippers being born. Then when he uses us for this glorious eternal purpose, we are blown away and come back to him, not just worshipping him for the wonderful God he is but praising him for the wonderful things he does. I believe that such a way of life is the most exciting one in the world!

Our touchstone scriptures at *The Message* are Isaiah 43:18–21 which go like this: *'Forget the former things; do not dwell on the past. See, I am doing a new thing! Now it springs up; do you not perceive it? I am making a way in the desert and streams in the wasteland. The wild animals honour me, the jackals and the owls, because I provide water in the desert and streams in the wasteland, to give drink to my people, my chosen, the people I formed for myself that they may proclaim my praise.'*

Right at the start of this whole adventure, God spoke to us through these verses and said that that's what he wants to do – to bring rivers of life rushing into Manchester, which in many ways spiritually is a desert place. You probably know that Europe is the only continent in the world where Christianity isn't growing, and in terms of decline, hardly anywhere is as bad as the north-west of England, so that's where we decided Jesus should be. Not just in Manchester, however, but with the toughest people and in the toughest places in Manchester – in other words, with the teenagers who are the biggest of the church's problems and in the inner city, where so many of the social ills of our society seem to be concentrated. I firmly believe that as we push on with the dream of rivers in the desert places, and as these strongholds are broken, blessings will be poured upon the whole city and, I'm arrogant enough to believe, the whole nation will be blessed.

The bit of these verses that I've never really spotted until recently is at the end in verse 21. *Can't you see that that's what God wants to do? Raise up worshippers!* There are people all over Manchester who have been formed to proclaim the praise of our God. Our great joy and privilege is to introduce him to them and watch them gain the dignity and significance that comes from being chosen by God to be a worshipper and used by him to introduce others to this exciting life.

Planet Life is our regular monthly worship service, which has grown into the largest in Europe, with around a couple of thousand eager worshippers regularly attending. We try and pack the programme with loads of DJs, worship leaders, bands, preachers and stuff. Invariably it runs over time and we are flapping around backstage trying to decide which bits to cut out. Last December, however, something bizarre happened. I'd finished my preach and the programme was running 20 minutes short. I thought the young people might feel a bit ripped off if we finished early so I said to our guest band *Yfriday*, and to the Tribe, 'Just go out and lead some worship.' I chucked them out on to the stage and hoped for the best. They absolutely rocked it and the atmosphere was electric as we finished the evening with a huge shout of praise. A bit later, I said to Ken, the lead singer from *Yfriday*, 'I don't know where that twenty minutes came from; that's never happened before.' He replied, 'It was as if the Lord stretched the programme and said "I want to be praised."'And he does and he will be, and it is only as we really become worshippers that we can make sense of who we are and who he is, and get a sense of the awesome truth that he, the almighty God of all creation, wants to partner us in this fantastic salvation business.

Light of the World

In John 8:12, Jesus makes this outrageous statement: 'I am the light of the world. Whoever follows me will never walk in darkness, but will have the light of life.' Jesus said 'I am I AM, the light of the world,' or, in other words, 'I am Yahweh, the light of the world.' Yahweh, or 'I am', was the name God had given himself in the Old Testament in Exodus 3:14. It is a name so holy to religious Jews that they will not even speak it. No wonder they wanted to kill him when he said this and, in saying it, claimed that he was Yahweh in the flesh. They knew that the Psalms had described Yahweh as 'My Light', but here was a mortal man claiming to be equal with God. Make no mistake, that is exactly what Jesus claimed and exactly what the New Testament writers and all real Christians have claimed ever since – Jesus is God. He is THE light of the world. How anyone can read the New Testament and say otherwise beats me. Romans 9:5 says 'Christ is God forever praised'. Hebrews 1:8 says about Jesus, 'Your throne, O God, lasts forever' – and so it goes on. So Jesus is God and as such, he knows how to squeeze the juice out of life and can say, in all seriousness, 'whoever follows me will never walk in darkness but will have the light of life'.

I've seen it time and again – the light of Jesus shining into dark hearts and lives and utterly transforming them. Among my closest friends are ex-drug addicts and convicts, alcoholics and people who have been horribly sexually abused. They have all had the light of Jesus shine in their hearts. He is the light of the world, and the darkness, no matter how dark, cannot overcome him.

Jesus also said something in Matthew 5:14–16 that was probably even more outrageous: 'You are the light of the world.' Jesus didn't just say, 'I am the light of the world'; he said, 'You are the light of the world.' 'You' means all Christians everywhere. We are the light of the world. Something amazing happened when Jesus died on the cross and rose again, conquering sin and death once and for all. The Jewish temple, one of the wonders of the ancient world, became defunct. For over a thousand years, it had been the centre of the Jewish faith. Every year, for the people's sins, the high priest sacrificed a goat and sprinkled blood on the mercy seat in the Holy of Holies where God dwelt. The Holy of Holies was protected by a richly embroidered 80-foot-high curtain, and before the High Priest entered he would go through an incredibly complicated rigmarole of fasting, praying and smearing himself with blood. The Holy of Holies would be filled with smoke and he would enter the presence of God bowed down and with a rope tied around his ankle so that if he died, he could be dragged out.

When the disciples drew Jesus' attention to the magnificence of the temple building, I'm sure they were thinking he would be impressed. But Jesus looked at them and said 'soon not one stone will be left on another'. I'm sure that for Jesus to say to the disciples that the temple, including the Holy of Holies, would be destroyed was almost as bad as blasphemy. But Jesus' words came true. He died on the cross and as he shouted with a loud voice, 'It is accomplished', meaning, 'I've done it: I've paid the price once and for all,' the curtain was torn in two from top to bottom (I like that!). It was picture language from God saying, 'I'm out of here. I've broken loose. No longer will I dwell in temples made by human hands but from now on, I'm going to live in people's hearts and reveal myself through them.'

As you know, Jesus then rose from the dead and conquered death, once and for all. He walked around for about six weeks, then got his disciples together on a hillside and said something amazing. 'As the Father sent me, so I am sending you.' Then he breathed on them and said, 'Receive the Holy Spirit.'

That's it! Staggering as it is to take in, we are sent as Jesus was sent. We are to do the work that Jesus would do if he were walking around in our Nike trainers. We are the light of the world. We are all God has. I don't know why he's done it this way – apart from the fact that he loves us and wants us to know the incredible joy of being filled with him and used by him – but the scary truth is also that if we don't let our light shine, the world will be a dark place.

That's why Jesus is so passionate that we don't hide our light under a bowl. Sometimes I think our church buildings and our meetings can be like a big bowl that we slap over the light as we all get together shining brightly with other people who are in the light when the light is meant to be shining in the darkness, 'so that men may see your good deeds and praise your father in heaven' (Matt 5:16). There it is again. God *will* be praised.

It really is time for an army of young evangelists to hit the streets, letting their lights shine and not giving up until our God gets the praise he deserves in this nation.

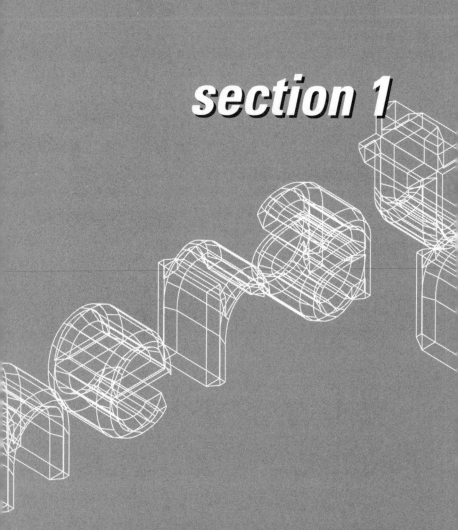

section 1

generation
rising

Back in November 2001, two stories ran almost parallel in the *Manchester Evening News*. They were both big pieces, and both involved great young people who we've been working with here in the city. One was a story overflowing with hope and positivity, the other a heart-breaking tragedy.

Charles, a bright young skater who loves God, was pictured pulling a fancy trick up in the air at the grand opening of the Skate Park which he has pioneered to reach out to the mosher subculture in Manchester's Northern Quarter. Jenny, a fun-loving schoolgirl on the fringe of Salford's EDEN project was described in the past tense. She had been viciously attacked by another girl with a knife and had died from wounds to her neck, just yards from Charles' door.

I've always hated that, 'what if you leave this place tonight and get run over by a bus?' approach to evangelism, but Jenny's short life story has reminded me in an all-too-real way that we cannot allow ourselves to become a generation who treat our faith like a leisurely stroll. Some serious acceleration is required. For this generation, life is a tightrope walk. As if simply maintaining some kind of balance is not difficult enough, there is continuous commotion and distraction all around. Where to look? What voice to listen to? What's the next step?

Guys like Charles demonstrate the massive human potential which God is desperate to raise up. His eye sees every one of the 2.3 billion Global Village citizens aged eighteen or under; in every way, they are a generation rising. We need to realise that his heart breaks when that generation sinks invisibly away. Jenny's premature silence speaks. Fellow travellers of this third millennium since Christ, please take seriously this time of opportunity and danger. Andy and I do. That's why we set up *Xcelerate*. We've looked around our city and seen a culture full of new germs resistant to past remedies. Our call is to breed a brave new strain of young evangelists. We hope that the programme works like a hypodermic shot of adrenaline in the heart, stepping up the beat for the lost. That's our desire for this book too.

Count to three, this won't hurt a bit...

what's so urgent about evangelism?

There are three kinds of people in the world.
There are those who make things happen.
There are those who watch things happen.
And there are those who say, 'What happened?'

Before Opening Mouth – Engage Brain!

Ask anyone where I'm from and ninety-nine times out of a hundred, you'll get the reply, 'Manchester'. But that's not strictly true, I'm only really half Manc – on my mum's side. My dad comes from Leeds, which makes for some interesting 'extended family dynamics'! The first eighteen years of my life were spent in the scruffy little towns of north-east Derbyshire. I've heard the area described as 'bandit country'... all the people on one side of the street would support Derby County and all the people on the other side would support Nottingham Forest. You didn't want to get caught on the wrong side of the street after the sun had gone down...

Our town centre consisted of two intersecting roads with traffic lights and a statue, a bronze war memorial greened with age – a soldier protecting an anxious little boy. Around this fairly busy little intersection was a cluster of four or five pubs, empty five days a week but crammed full of all sorts of characters on Friday and Saturday nights. Since the age of fourteen or fifteen, this unknown corner of the world had become the centre of my weekend universe. Now, at the age of sixteen, I was a well-known face – up for a slice of whatever action the evening would serve up for us.

It had been a hot summer Friday, and the *Red Lion* had been filling up since early afternoon with lads knocking off work early from the local factories. By nine o'clock every pub was heaving, right out onto the street. Fed up with the endless repetition of the Stone Roses' 'Fool's Gold' in the *Four Horseshoes*, a few of the lads and I decided to make a move across the road to the next watering hole. We stepped out boisterously and it was in that moment, right as we stepped out into the traffic that, in earshot of the whole town I had the overwhelming urge to shout. I looked up as the traffic lights turned red, took a deep breath and cried out at the top of my voice... 'NO POLL TAX!'

You don't need a degree in British political history to know that there was no issue in 1990 that got the pulses of the populous racing more than the Poll Tax fiasco. People all over the nation had been refusing to pay up, even under the threat of fines and imprisonment. Maybe I should have thought of that before letting the cheeky jibe out of my mouth?

Almost simultaneously, an echo came from the direction of one of the other pubs, then another from behind me. A cheer went up into the dimming sky and all

The primal chorus was now accompanied by the sound of breaking glass and sirens approaching from somewhere in the distance.

eyes were on Wilson and Co. standing in the middle of the road wearing pretty smug expressions. We looked each other and with symphonic timing broke out into a repeat chorus of 'NO POLL TAX! NO POLL TAX! NO POLL TAX!', fists punching the air. One by one, as we continued the chant, we began to sit down on the warm tarmac, attracting nervous hoots from the passing vehicles, swerving to avoid our high jinks.

In less than a minute, the air was filled with hundreds of voices, and the pubs began emptying as curious revellers became spontaneous demonstrators. Our little cluster in the middle of the road seemed to develop a gravitational force and soon the whole street was full. Cars were forced to stop and as they did, so did I. I glanced around in disbelief at the chaotic scenes and realised that something had begun that wasn't about to end in a hurry. I got to my feet and squeezed to the edge of the road, up the steps of our destination pub and into the relative shelter of its doorway, just as the first pint pot flew up into the air, bounced off a car bonnet and shattered to a huge cheer.

'NO POLL TAX! NO POLL TAX! NO POLL TAX!' The primal chorus was now accompanied by the sound of breaking glass and sirens approaching from somewhere in the distance.

It took the police almost an hour to bring the situation under control, and thankfully, there were only a few arrests and no serious injuries. A few weeks later Thatcher was out, Saddam was at large and the whole thing was forgotten, except by me. I have never forgotten the power of words and I'll never again take lightly the ability of the one to affect the destiny of the many.

Since we launched *Xcelerate* and began pouring in serious time with young guys and girls passionate about Jesus, one thing has become crystal clear. Every day God gives us on this planet is packed with opportunity. If you were to start counting tomorrow, you'd probably recognise before lunchtime a hundred ways the world offers you to compromise your relationship with God and your witness for him. Living in that world is tiring and draining, like pedalling your bike up a steep hill. Together with the guys and girls on our programme, we're learning to live above that, to live in the parallel world where God can reveal a hundred ways to honour him and make him known – before you've brushed your teeth!

It's worth mentioning that we've been through such times of opportunity, we've had to come up with new words to describe things that were beginning to happen to us! We invented a new phrase – you can have it for free – God Prod! It's not in any dictionary, not even the trusty *Unger's Bible Dictionary*, but if it were, it might be defined like this:

God Prod: a moment of time within time where God directly interrupts the daily routine of one of his children, bringing a high state of awareness towards an imminent human interaction.

That's the academic way of putting it. A more down to earth description might be, *'A Holy Spirit kick up the bum!'*

Evangelism is urgent – urgent every minute of every day. There is an urgency of opportunity. God wants to use you to be significant in someone's life today. The bonus ball, when you start living with an eye for God's opportunities rather than the world's temptations, is that God grows his children through opportunity. There are many Christian training programs and Year Outs around where young people are used like cheap labour, spending all day licking envelopes and making cups of tea for 'the ministry', to teach them how to be a 'servant'. At *Xcelerate*, we'd contend with that. There's a difference between being a servant and becoming servile. God needs people who will serve the poor and the broken, serve the lost and the confused, serve the oppressed and the hurting. For that you need every ounce of initiative, humility and stamina that you've got, because in every street of every town and every city right across this land, there are opportunities to make a difference. Opportunity will knock more than once, but the first knock is the loudest.

Ask God to open your eyes and ears to the opportunities around you today.

Short-Changed by Your Creator?

Have you ever been shopping and returned to find your pocket considerably emptier than you expected? You mentally retrace your steps…

'So, I got two pints of milk, a loaf of bread, a tin of spaghetti hoops, a frozen pizza and a Curly Wurly… I paid with a twenty… and I've got six quid left? They've ripped me off!!!'

Evangelism is urgent – urgent every minute of every day.

A toxic blend of anger and disappointment races from your toes to your ears and you spend the next three hours in a mood with everyone. You decide to go back to the shop, after rehearsing your speech in the mirror once or twice to boost your confidence. With a deep breath you step through the automatic door and instantly recognise the cashier. Like an express train, you will not be diverted, until you notice the handy little name badge sitting proudly on her apron. It says 'GOD', next to three gold stars and a little smiley face.

The argument has raged for centuries and I don't expect to end it here, but is everyone born on this planet a potential citizen of heaven? Or is there simply a predetermined number designed and delivered by God with the soul capacity for a relationship with him? Both corners of the debate carry heavyweight spiritual clout into the ring but it's the fact that they're scrapping at all that saddens me. My personal experience is that God does not short-change people. I've met people hostile to the gospel who, within thirty minutes, have softened up to the extent that they'll begin to pray, even on occasion willing to surrender their lives totally to Jesus. Yet I hold that in tension with all the friends and family for who I still pray passionately for, sometimes in faith, sometimes wondering if they've actually got the right wiring to 'connect' with God at all.

By the age of twenty, I'd traded in my wild nights on the town for the much safer option of staying in and getting totally stoned. Most of those nights are just a smoky haze hidden somewhere deep in the archives of my brain. However, one night has taken on special significance for me. Let me paint the picture and I think you'll get the point.

Imagine three young guys. They think they are the epitome of cool, but really they're hiding away from a world they've forgotten how to relate to. Three-thirty in the morning, in a leafy Manchester suburb, being careful not to burn holes in their mate's mum's new sofa. Hardly the stuff of *Trainspotting* chic. I dimp out another spliff, sit back heavily into the armchair and exhale the universal dopehead declaration, 'I'm wasted…' It had been said a thousand times but this time, the words seemed to hang in the smoky air. They played back in my head like the confession of a cornered criminal.

'I'm wasted…' The lights come on in my shadowy mind.

'I'm wasted…'

There is so much possibility in this vast world, so much potential in this young body. Too much to be wasted by this lifestyle, too much to be wasted in this room.

One of my favourite songs is, 'Open the eyes of my heart, Lord… I want to see you.' One of my most frequent prayers is, 'Open the eyes of my heart Lord… I want to see what you see.' Sometimes I'll walk through the streets of Manchester and watch the people around me scurrying here and there in the tramlines of their private worlds. My heart pounds inside my chest and I find myself imagining destinies for individuals who walk by.

This girl in the puffa jacket could be leading kids in worship within a year. That old Jamaican fella selling newspapers may be the instrument for God to flood blessing through three generations of his family. This guy sitting at the traffic lights in his shiny new Saab might be God's man to bring righteous kingdom values into the greedy sales world.

'Come on, Lord, make a way,' my heart screams.

And the Lord replies, 'Go on then, talk to them.'

'God, how?'

'I've given you a brain, haven't I? Use it!'

There is an urgency of potential all around us. I wish Manchester were an exception, that I could get in my car one morning and drive down the M6 to Birmingham and find the city centre packed with office workers fulfilled in their God-given destinies or whiz along the M62 to the council estates of Bradford and meet street after street of mums and dads living out their purpose for life. But that's not the world we live in. Not yet. Martyred missionary Jim Elliot described his quest to reach the unreached tribes of the Amazon as 'living to the hilt'. I don't think that we can take on the mission to reach the tribes on our doorstep any less enthusiastically. We must evangelise, yes, to save people from a wasted eternity, but much more urgent than that, save them from a wasted life.

Looking Through the Wrong End of the Telescope

During the 2001 New Year celebrations, I was in Washington DC. My sister, Rebekah, had unexpectedly decided to tie the knot with her long-term American boyfriend and had politely given the family three weeks' notice. The day after Boxing Day, we all got up painfully early and made our weary way to Manchester Airport's Terminal One, kept in the land of the living by the taxi driver's extra loud reggae/soul collection. It wasn't until we began to come round at about thirty thousand feet that we began to realise that we had no idea what the next week had in store for us. Rebekah is a fantastic girl and we all love her big time, but we knew in the back of our minds that her proven independent spirit, combined with a feminist persuasion developed at University, was set to make this a very different kind of wedding.

When we touched down and met up with the future in-laws, it was confirmed that yes, it was going to be a church wedding, with a 'proper' vicar, dog collar, vestments, the full monty. The happy couple had decided, however, not to hold the event in the sanctuary, but under the Christmas tree in the entrance hall, just a small intimate gathering. Great. We could all picture that, classic with a twist. Then came the matter of the rings.

'Oh, we're not really bothered about rings…' –Some kind of conscientious objection to the symbolism? Maybe?

' …but we'll be exchanging items of personal meaning…'

Well, that adds a touch of spice, a little surprise for us all to look forward to on the day.

'…and I don't want Dad to give me away.'

Hold on. Did I just hear what I think I heard?

It took about twenty-four hours for the full impact of that final adjustment to the traditional wedding ceremony to sink in. It bothered me, really deeply, I talked about it at length with my wife Grace. For her, being 'given away' by her father had been one of the most moving moments of the whole day, and I certainly felt the sincere transfer of trust and care to me from the man who had loved her since the day she drew her first breath. Why would Rebekah feel so strongly about erasing this part of the occasion? I couldn't really understand it, none of us could. We needed to talk.

The following day, we were in our hotel room and the phone rang – I picked it up and responded to my sister's chirpy greeting. We began small-talking about some of the wedding details, but this whole Dad thing was so heavy on my heart that I had to bring it up. Not the world's most skilled conversationalist, I couldn't see how to get from this place of chit-chat to the real point. Life doesn't give us a script for such moments.

'Bek, errrm, you know this thing about dropping Dad out of the service… what's all that about? Help me out, I'm having trouble understanding…'

I chewed on a flaky bit of my lip and gripped the phone a little too tightly as the girl I grew up with and thought I knew so well explained to me that she was not a piece of property to be passed on from one male to another. I didn't know what to say. I wasn't prepared, and talking off the top of my head usually does more harm than good. I wound up the conversation by saying:

'Grace and I would love to chat with you some more about this: would that be okay? I don't want to change your mind but I do think we might be able to help you see this from another perspective.'

I put the handset back in the cradle and put my head in my hands. Grace laid her hand on my shoulder and gave me one of those wonderfully reassuring smiles that she does really well. It's hard to describe the emotions that were stirring inside… disappointment, frustration, perhaps even anger, but not directed towards my sister. No, towards the world we inhabit together which constantly distorts what is good and right, even inside the minds of the coolest, most intelligent, well-adjusted people. That's where the frustration comes in. As a professional problem solver, I know I need to be able to pinpoint the source of an issue to deal with it – but how do you begin to correct a global, invisible thought

*If you were expecting
the Xcelerate course
syllabus in ten easy
lessons, then sorry,
this isn't it. What you
are holding in your
hands is our attempt
to communicate to
you what we have in
our hearts for this
generation – the
passion we try to pass
on to every person we
take on in Xcelerate.*

system corrupt to the core? How do you tell someone that they're looking through the wrong end of the telescope?

There is an urgency for truth. Our politicians, our educators, our media, yes, even 'the church' daily show their desperate desire to feed warped data into our open ears. In recent years, the best-selling Christian books and most avidly watched Christian TV shows seem to promote the central theme 'God wants you to be selfish!' I recently heard of a Christian who had become a Muslim. His reasoning was that in the Church of Christ, which is a cult, God revolves around the individual, yet in Islam the individual revolves around God. What has happened to the truth? The new generation of evangelists needs to journey with this question and find some solid ground. You don't have to become a professor of post-rapture-transmogrification, but hurry up and get a grip of foundation truth. Be sure of its standard and confident of its effectiveness in this post-modern realm of smoke and mirrors. People need truth today more than ever before. Swallowing the truth of God's infinite goodness and grace expressed to us in Jesus Christ is *the* only way out of this matrix.

This book is designed to help you on that truth journey. If you were expecting the *Xcelerate* course syllabus in ten easy lessons, then sorry, this isn't it. What you are holding in your hands is our attempt to communicate to you what we have in our hearts for this generation – the passion we try to pass on to every person we take on in *Xcelerate*. We hope that your eyes will get opened to the opportunities surrounding you every day. We hope to inspire you about the potential God has born inside you. We hope to help you to decode the messages crowding your mind in your urgent search for truth.

chapter one

chapter two

somethin'
in the flava

I hear... and I forget
I see... and I remember
I do... and I understand

Confucius

Call Centre Syndrome

If you've ever worked for a call centre, which, apparently, ten per cent of the population have done, you'll be able to relate to me as I begin to map out this chapter. If you've worked in sales I think you'll be with me, too. There is the profound temptation to switch to auto-speak mode and begin regurgitating information which has been rattled out a thousand times before. It's like when you get back from that fortnight in Tenerife with your lovely tan then everyone you meet for the next three weeks asks you the same question:

'So, how was your holiday then?'

By the sixtieth time you've been asked, all the exciting stories have been edited down to a one-second, 'Yeah, nice.'

I promise you that in this chapter, no matter how many times I've talked about it before, I'm going to give you the best explanation of all the stuff we do here in Manchester, why we do it and how it all fits together.

Redecorating

Recently we went through a bit of a mini-revolution back at the office. For years and years, we'd had a set of horrendously cheesy posters framed on the wall of our rather tatty meeting/prayer room. They had a curious two-tone screen print effect and depicted giddy children and well-groomed parents bearing slogans like,

'Please do attend church on Sunday!'

'Sunday School is Splendid!'

and 'Christians have nice teeth and don't smell'.

For us, the posters were a post-modern ironic statement reminding us of our uphill pedal to drag the church into the real world – and a bit of a laugh. Sadly, about ninety per cent of our visitors didn't see the funny side. It's always the way with 'in jokes', they just didn't get it. Many respected Christian leaders would come in and sit down on the sofa, then glance up at the wall in disbelief. You could almost hear their brains grinding with confusion...

'Did I take the right turning off the M60? Is this the headquarters of *The World Wide Message Tribe* or have I accidentally ended up at *Holy Quiche Bakers for Jesus?*'

We had to get rid. Now, in their place, we have three crisp, glossy pieces of artwork designed by our webmaster Joe Kizlauskas. His brief was to create some images to remind us of the commission God has given us to our city.

Without getting too philosophical about changing a few pictures on a wall, I do believe that, by doing so, we have marked a watershed in our ministry and highlighted an important value in our work. It's a statement about attitude and prevailing mindset. Maybe once upon a time, back in the early days, our motivation was a reaction against the perceived irrelevance and failure of the previous generation. But you can't build a lasting work for God on such shaky foundations. Movements merely reacting *against* something and never acting *for* something will eventually run out of steam and themselves become monuments. Like the great prophet Isaiah says, 'Forget the former things: do not dwell in the past.'

Instead, do all you can to get a glimpse of the future that your life is flowing towards. You must. It's essential. Spend time daily listening to God. Ask him to open your eyes to the world around you. Ask him to show you what he sees. Look with compassion on 'the human now' and search for a snapshot of completion in 'the divine present'. To meet the needs of this planet, we need to have God's perspective. He has the ability to see his creation not just as we do in the frustration and futility of its fallen state but in the fullness and glory of its restoration.

That fullness and restoration is what we've begun to see as we've meditated on the words of God, 'See, I am doing a new thing... I am making a way...' What incredibly rich words – so much hope, complete confidence. See, his demand for our attention. *I Am*, the almighty God's personal commitment. *Doing* and *Making*, the words of urgent, immediate action. *A New Thing – a Way*, a refreshing journey leading to deeper knowledge of his goodness and grace. Those are the words that now welcome visitors at our HQ because those are the words that we are carrying in our hearts. When you see them written over photographs of young people trapped on the forgotten streets of Salford, they take on a new dimension of power – faith. We can't see right now what we know is possible in God, but we are certain that we're accelerating towards the day when we *will* see it.

Stealing Parables

As a ministry, we send out a quarterly newsletter to about twenty thousand *Message* supporters around the world. A recent edition left me feeling pretty embarrassed. You see Andy writes a little editorial for each issue called 'Andy's Rant' and in this particular rant he had picked up on something I had shared in a prayer meeting. It was about how the illustrations of salt and light, which Jesus uses in Matthew 5, tie in with the parables of the yeast and the mustard seed in Luke 13. The point was that as God's people in our city, we should be, like salt or yeast, an invisible influence on the nature of our society, but at the same time we are to stand out and be seen like a lamp on a stand or a tree in a garden. You'd have a job finding a better picture for our work here in Manchester.

Of course, there's nothing immediately embarrassing about any of that, only that what Andy didn't know, when he gave me credit for it, was that I'd nicked the revelation from my pastor who had preached on it the previous Sunday! That might have been the end of the matter, but having traced it back to him, I discovered that he had also stolen it from EA President Joel Edwards who was in town doing one of those 'Gee up the churches' tours. What goes around comes around, they say. Let's have a closer look at the ins and outs of how *Message* brand salt finds its saltiness and how *Message* brand light gets its brightness. Focus... this is where it gets technical.

The Umbrella

chapter two

Since we kicked off our work with a city-wide mission in 1988, *The Message* has always been pioneering cutting-edge youth initiatives. *The Message* charity was formally registered as *The Message to Schools Trust* in 1992. Not surprisingly, the sole project of the charity was to work in Manchester high schools, particularly alongside RE departments, to communicate the Christian message to young people in a way that was relevant and interesting. At the time, the organisation employed one full-time member of staff with a guitar and a Ford Cortina! The annual turnover was about £20,000. The numbers have gone into orbit since then but *The Message* still exists to serve young people everyday across Greater Manchester. We still aim to communicate and demonstrate the Christian faith relevantly. The work remains firmly rooted in schools, but the task has broadened to reach out to young people with many different needs in many different settings through all possible means.

From the small beginnings, *The Message Trust* umbrella has opened up into a charitable company limited by guarantee, for those of you who are familiar with corporate law! The turnover hovers around a scary £1 million. People often ask where the cash comes from and the truth is that we often end up praying in the money to pay the bills and the wages at the end of the month. Provision usually comes by the regular giving of many individuals and local churches, plus a number of charitable trusts. We currently have almost fifty staff on the payroll, who work on various projects, alongside dozens of committed volunteers. All have a long-term commitment to the human regeneration of Manchester's needy inner city areas, with a focus on working with young people, even if they spend all day answering phones in the office. The unified desire is to see every young person in Greater Manchester being presented with opportunities to achieve their full potential in every area of life. We share the belief with millions all around the world that the only real way to get there is through a personal relationship with Jesus.

Under the shade of this expanding umbrella live six clearly definable, yet frequently overlapping ministries: *The Tribe, Planet Life, EDEN, EDEN Bus Ministry, The LifeCentre* and *Xcelerate*.

The work of our Trust is enhanced and enabled no end by working partnerships with many diverse organisations; for example, Greater Manchester Police, Salford City Council, The Church of England, The Salvation Army, The Shaftesbury Society, The Luis Palau Evangelistic Association, *Open Hands International, Operation Christmas Child* and *Soul Survivor*.

The World Wide Message Tribe

…which we still get called, to our great annoyance, was formed in 1991, specifically to reach into Manchester high schools. Mark Pennells, vocalist and musician, joined forces with our man Andy Hawthorne, at the time a wide boy entrepreneur in the fashion industry. The dynamic duo met at a music event and instantly realised that they shared a vision for reaching a new generation with the good news of Jesus Christ. The vision quickly found shape and direction, as Mark and Andy began preaching and performing in local schools. Results were immediate and encouraging, as the combination of dance music and evangelism took hold but you'll have to read Andy's book *Mad for Jesus* to hear the whole story of those crazy years.

That's enough of the history, as the current story is equally exciting – the story of *The Tribe*. It features long-serving members Tim Owen, Lindzi West and Emma Owen, who have now been joined by Quintin Delport and George Mhondera, ex-members of the South African band *MiC*. Christmas 2001 saw the release of their first album together called *Take Back the Beat* which was quickly followed up by cut-price concept-linked CD discipleship resource, *The Beat Goes On*. Even with new members coming and going, *The Tribe*, as they are now officially titled, are still faithful to their original calling of working in Manchester. You have to concede that this is pretty staggering, considering their success on American Top 40 radio with *The Real Thing*, headlining music festivals all over Europe, three Gospel Music Association Dove Awards, two celebrated five-week tours of the US and five number one Christian Radio singles!

> Christianity is shown in its true light as a living and relevant faith.

The work of *The Tribe* has always been focused around presenting the Christian message to young people in Manchester's high schools in a way to which the pupils can relate. RE is often seen by pupils as being irrelevant and boring, regardless of how hard staff try to make the lessons stimulating and interesting. As outsiders coming into a school, *The Tribe* find it easier to get the pupils' attention, if only through the curiosity factor provoked by the clothes and the haircuts. Their fast-moving style and the use of banging loud music also helps! Clearly there is a certain amount of 'entertainment' in the presentation but there is also well-planned teaching content in each lesson. Facts about Christianity are presented and ethical dilemmas posed. *Tribe* members share their stories and experiences, allowing time for kids to respond with 'off the cuff' questions. For the week that the team is in the school, Christianity is shown in its true light as a living and relevant faith. Of course, the pupils are encouraged to think about it for themselves.

On top of this, we try to make sure that there's a Friday evening gig for as many kids as we can legally squeeze into the hall. The music is pumping, the lights are spinning and the gospel is explained with the help of a few anecdotes from the lives of *The Tribe*. Anyone present who wants to respond to God or just to ask a few more questions can connect with either the team or one of the volunteers at the end of the concert.

It's worth mentioning that, as well as the schools gigs, *The Tribe* perform every month at *Planet Life*, our regular monthly celebration bash with DJs, bands and speakers. Young people met in schools, plus youth groups from miles around can have another chance to hear more about the gospel and experience an atmosphere of worship. *Planet Life* began in the dusty twilight of St Mary's Parish Church which sits at the traffic lights, the most exciting place in sleepy Cheadle village. Over the last five years, the numbers attending every month have increased so much that we've moved home twice, touching down in 1999 in the 2,500 seater Manchester Apollo Theatre. *Planet Life* has grown into the largest regular youth worship event in Europe. Young people come from all over Manchester and beyond to 'jump in the house' for their creator!

Could These People Raise Your House Price?

So read the headline in the Daily Telegraph. Above it was a huge picture of *The Tribe* in full flow at a *Planet Life* event. It turned out that the writer of the article was really getting at the *EDEN* phenomenon, our radical youthwork model of moving committed long-term workers back into the inner city. 'Bringing hope to the toughest parts of Manchester.' Maybe this is the right point to let you know, in case you hadn't spotted it already, that although this book draws much from the ethos and identity of *Xcelerate*, the Evangelists Training School, *Xcelerate* itself would not exist if it were not to serve the cause of *EDEN*. We make no bones about declaring publicly that *EDEN* is our most significant work. Because many people ask about it, here are some more facts.

To some, it's 'la-la land', but the fact is that churches are growing and crime is being reduced in some of the toughest areas of Manchester. We're convinced that *EDEN* has had a fair bit to do with this. The exciting vision was conceived in 1996, and the first *EDEN* project was born in 1997 on the sprawling South Manchester council estate of Wythenshawe, following two weeks of outreach by *The World Wide Message Tribe*. A partnership with King's Church, a local church already trying to reach out to the young people of the area, was the missing link in the discipleship chain which, until that point, ended at the end of a six-week *Get God* course. It was clear that a permanent presence was needed if the young people who had been contacted by the work were to be effectively helped on an ongoing basis. The aim of *EDEN* is to meet that challenge.

In 1997 we set to work recruiting a team of full-time and part-time workers whose work is now exclusively focused in the schools and on the streets of the *EDEN* areas. The brief, as always, is to communicate Christianity relevantly and effectively to the young people, presenting them, in this context, with varied opportunities to develop their skills, character and self-worth. Workers use music, sports, creative arts and anything else they can dream up to secure long-term mentoring relationships. Dozens of volunteer 'tent-making' missionaries have moved into Wythenshawe and joined this exciting venture. These guys and girls work during the day to earn a crust but are committed to living long-term in the inner city. They are active members of the local church, helping to run the youth work, befriending the young people in the areas in which they live. At every opportunity they get involved in running youth clubs and events, as well as reaching out on the streets as detached youth teams.

Following on from *EDEN* Wythenshawe, *The Message* now has five other *EDEN* projects up and running all based on the same model as in Wythenshawe. They are in Salford, Longsight, Openshaw, Swinton and Harpurhey. Get yourself on www.streetmap.co.uk if those names don't mean anything to you! The big picture is a vision to recruit a 'Gideon's Army' of three hundred workers for the inner city of Manchester and to establish ten *EDEN* projects city-wide, and we're well on the way to seeing this exciting vision fulfilled. Your geographical knowledge of the North West may break down somewhere round about here but try and stick with it. Plans include planting future *EDEN* projects into Failsworth, North Manchester – one of the most deprived wards in Britain, with unemployment running at over 25% (1991) and the worst teenage pregnancy rate in Europe (1995). Hattersley, East Manchester – a desperately needy inner-city overspill estate with youth unemployment of 34% and high levels of drug abuse amongst young people.

We also hope to launch *EDEN* projects soon in Oldham and Moss Side, where we will need great skill and anointing in facing up to racial issues that we don't have a lot of experience in. The evidence we have so far shows that long-term relationships are the key to any work with young people, however difficult the area may seem on the surface. Take, for instance, the team of thirty *EDEN* workers living in the troubled Langworthy area of Salford. 'Well dodgy', some would say, but the workers love the place and are finding real acceptance into the community. We have a special pilot project there to resource them better for their work; it's the *LifeCentre,* a facility to complement their existing schools and detached youthwork.

chapter
two

The LifeCentre

I think this project has a great name which sums up a great new concept in youth and community provision. The physical *LifeCentre* building is a facility which serves the community by advising, caring, training and providing opportunities for young people who are marginalised by society. It was opened in summer 2000 as one of the sustainable social action projects delivered by *Soul Survivor – The Message 2000*. It's radical, creative and is proving a key resource in representing the love and life of Jesus right in the heart of Salford.

Administratively, the *LifeCentre* is run by *The Message* in partnership with two other charities. There's the Shaftesbury Society, a well-respected social action agency, with 150 years experience, and *Open Hands International*, who provide care, education, accommodation, and stuff, like schools and orphanages in India. In an area like Salford, recognised as somewhere that has really suffered from high levels of crime, youth unemployment and poverty, the *LifeCentre* is perfectly placed to meet the real needs. Moreover, each young person we come into contact with can be given the opportunity to participate in local church.

The *LifeCentre's* ethos is very much one of being an enabler, rather than an expert who comes in and takes over. In many ways, local people are best placed to address their own needs. This means we encourage local community groups to work with the young people of their own areas. We believe that by empowering young people with a positive perception of themselves by finding their true worth in God, we can increase their social skills and confidence. It's important to build within them a strong foundation of Christian values. The scope of work is broad, stretching from twelve- to twenty-five-year olds. A buzzing youth café acts as an access point to practical help in the form of training, IT resources, sports and leisure activities, arts and crafts workshops, counselling services, financial guidance, and HIV, pregnancy and sexual health education. Above all The *LifeCentre* is a place where young people can find personal expression and be listened to without prejudice.

From Double Decker Buses to Xcelerators

The *EDEN* Buses are 'state-of the-art' mobile youth resources working in all the *EDEN* areas day in, day out. Both are excellent tools for the early stages of relational evangelism work. Inside an *EDEN* bus you could be forgiven for thinking 'Am I in The *LifeCentre*?' and in fact, the same interior design team worked on both. There's serious theory and method at work here, though, not just big budget extravagance. The same metallic fixtures and fittings of bus and *LifeCentre* become familiar to the kids, as do the faces of the team who serve day in, day out, to keep the word literally on the street. There are bus drivers, management staff, *EDEN* workers, and last but not least, the *Xcelerate* trainees. Yes, let's spend a bit of time looking at what goes into making them the tremendous blessing that they are.

In the summer of 2000, it was our pleasure to introduce *Xcelerate*, the latest addition to the work of *The Message* in Manchester. *Xcelerate* provides a top-notch training facility through which our vision, passion and values can be passed on to a new generation. We invited the 10,000 punters who'd spent five days at *Message 2000* to come back for five months. About forty of them decided that they would.

We set out some simple aims:
1. To identify gifted young evangelists, no matter how raw
2. To guide them through an intense twenty-week course designed to develop their knowledge, skills, character and motivation
3. To release them into a lifetime of effective ministry in the power of the Holy Spirit

The name *Xcelerate* came from a genuine desire to accelerate young Christian outreach workers in every area of their life, coming from the point of view that who you are is more important than what you do. *Xcelerate* contains all the basic elements of Christian outreach work including local church life, varied experience of practical placements, prayer, worship, pastoral care and, of course, solid Bible teaching. We hope we've created something fresh, creative and relevant for the twenty-first century. Our funky base in the heart of Manchester's City Centre *Uni-Land* tries to express that through its decor (must be seen to be believed!).

The teaching is broken up into weekly themes, supplemented by a simple reading programme and lots of scary verbal assignments.

Weeks 1–10:   The Gospels – the character of Jesus, being a disciple
Weeks 11–20:   The Acts – the work of the Holy Spirit, the purpose of the church

A typical 'week' runs from Monday to Friday and comprises teaching in the mornings and practical / pastoral activities in the afternoons. Weekends combine church life, free time and opportunities to serve on local initiatives. Each trainee's timetable is unique and made up of small folio units. There will always be practical training on the 'front line' through challenging placements. All the *EDEN* projects are involved as well as *The LifeCentre* and *Planet Life*. We send *Xcelerators* out on a number of outreach ministries to the homeless and into the local prisons. There are organised stints of mission throughout, particularly towards the end of every course.

Everyone who completes the course receives *The Message Certificate in Evangelism* from Andy at a posh commissioning party with loads of food.

Staying Focussed

Life in *Messageland* can be, to quote a recent *Tribe* album, *Frantik*. With all that's going on, each member of the team has to be focussed on Jesus. Everybody is susceptible to becoming task-oriented. Andy and I are the worst offenders but we know all too well that when we take our eyes off Jesus, we find ourselves floundering in deep water. To ensure that we don't drift too far off course, Andy insists that the whole ministry drops anchor once a month so that we can seek God together. Through prayer, worship and sometimes even a bit of fasting we strive to catch the wind of his Spirit. Without that, all the cool stuff that you've read about in this chapter is utterly meaningless.

chapter
two

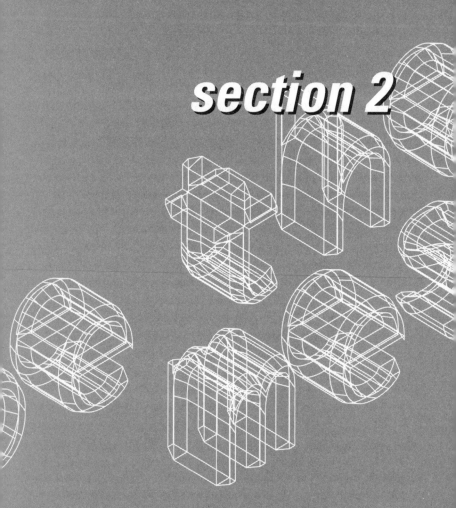

section 2

be the
message

You've heard of Mother Theresa. She died a few years ago but her legacy – the work she poured herself into in the slums of Calcutta – lives on strong. I've picked up a couple of first-hand stories from guys who had the privilege of meeting her in person.

Youth for Christ's director, Roy Crowne, told me about the time he met Mother Theresa. It left quite an impression on him. He was out in India with another guy; as part of their itinerary, they had prioritised the home in Calcutta for a special visit. As their host took them to meet the awesome little nun, a situation was just breaking. Through an interpreter, they listened to what was going on. A man riddled with horrific diseases had been brought in. He was at death's door, and stank as if he'd already passed through it. Mother Theresa was becoming insistent on a particular point of his treatment. Roy enquired as to what she felt so strongly about. The interpreter responded,

'This case is so bad that she will not let anyone else deal with it. She requests that she is given full responsibility for cleaning the body and preparing the patient for death. She wishes to give him dignity.'

As a leader of many, Roy was absolutely blown away that someone in a position of senior leadership should insist on undertaking what many would perceive as being the worst job. In reality, she was simply living out Christ's most profound teaching, that the greatest is in fact the servant of all.

Another great evangelist who we all know and love met Mother Theresa almost by accident. J. John found himself in her path as she entered a conference. Perhaps because he's a little guy as well, they made eye contact and she approached him.

'What's your name?' she asked.

'John,' he replied nervously, wondering what else he could say to qualify himself to this woman of such awesome reputation.

'Do you love Jesus, John?' she continued. But John couldn't say anything else. The power and the purity of the question had pierced his heart. Tears began to well up in his eyes. She'd put her finger right on the pulse of his relationship with God. In that moment, nothing else mattered. He knew there'd never be a time again when he'd have to use an introduction any more fancy than 'My name is John and I love Jesus.'

This section lingers on the theme of evangelism from

the perspective that an evangelist is who you are, not what you do. I hope it will inspire you to live evangelistically instead of settling for 'doing evangelism'.

extra ordinary
evangelists

The true way to be humble is not to stoop down until you are smaller than yourself, but to stand at your real height against some higher nature that will show what the real smallness of your greatness is.

Philip Brooks, writer of 'O little town of Bethlehem'

Lemmings

The first week we spend with any new batch of *Xcelerators* is dedicated to getting them to know one another, but also to getting them to know themselves. You can imagine the nervous scenes as they gather for the first time, twenty of them all nicely groomed and terribly polite, packed into the lounge at our house near the Manchester *Apollo*. We try really hard during the selection process to get a good mix of personalities. The end product can make for some really entertaining group dynamics and that's where the fun starts.

One of the first things we do is to test the boundaries of the strengths and weaknesses of the group. We employ various methods to this end: for instance, bright and early on the morning of Day 2, we'll pull up in the minibus and pile them all in for a magical mystery tour. A favourite spot of ours lies halfway between Buxton and Leek, just beyond the wonderfully-named 'Axe Edge'. It's a bleak, windswept place, populated by sheep, crows and utterly bonkers pensioners wrapped in *Gore-tex* tea cosies. We tend to fit right in (not).

Last time we were there, I had a new game to try out. I'd picked it up from a friend of mine who's doing a PhD in 'How to Embarrass People' at Lancaster Uni. The game is called 'Veil of Silence' – very mysterious. The idea is that you get your newly-formed group out into some dramatic landscape and get them to engage with it on a sensual level – sight, sound, smell and all that. Stimulation for body, mind and spirit. This is where the silence thing comes in. It's hard to get them to participate fully while they're all busy showing off and flirting with each other, so we 'put on the veil of silence'. And we really did put it on. I was amazed that everyone went for it – just a few sniggers and funny looks as we mimed picking up our cloaks and wrapping them around us. I silently positioned them, one by one, at thirty-foot intervals along the edge of the cliff and let them know that I'd be back for them in fifteen minutes.

It was only then that I noticed the rambling family striding up the rocky path towards us all, laughing, joking and enjoying the fresh Peak District air. I shrank back into a convenient crag as they appeared over the brow of the hill and stumbled into our game. The two young kids stopped dead in their tracks as they beheld the sight of twenty 'grown-ups' poised unnaturally, gazing into the sky. Mum and Dad quickly grabbed their hands and looked at each other in horror. I wasn't close enough to hear their whispers but if their body language was anything to go by, their conversation revolved around one horribly dark subject, *Mass Suicide!* Quick kids, leg it!

Fair play to our raw recruits, not one of them even flinched. The rambling family will have recovered from the trauma now and the kids are probably back in school. However, the incident did make me think about how weird our Christian faith must look to outsiders. Even when we think that we're living on the edge and being 'deliberately different', is it not true that we are just a curiosity to the world?

Even when we think that we're living on the edge and being 'deliberately different', is it not true that we are just a curiosity to the world?

To see the reality of this deliberately different conundrum being lived out for real, you'll have to visit one of our *EDEN* projects. The 150 young evangelists living as salt and yeast in the inner city of Manchester are faced daily with the challenge of living Jesus-centred lives in their communities without freaking everyone out and causing them to run a mile. These young evangelists come from pretty ordinary families. They have ordinary jobs and ordinary houses. They follow the example of a Jesus born in an ordinary manger in an ordinary stable in an ordinary town called Bethlehem. If you were to meet one of the guys or girls from an *EDEN* team, they'd probably get quite excited about the fact that Jesus found himself twelve ordinary mates and spent three years meeting ordinary people.

So if it's all so ordinary, why bother including it in a squashed-for-space book on evangelism? Well, precisely for that reason! Because it so clearly demonstrates God's heart to restore his relationship with the people he created. He didn't send a fax to earth, he sent *his* son. *EDEN* follows that example. Most of the team members have discarded comfy suburban homes, even promising careers and precious relationships to live among and reach out to ordinary people in Manchester. To the community around them who've never heard the gospel, they *become* the gospel. In a sense, you could describe their technique as 'word become flesh'. All the signs herald an end to old-fashioned 'Hit and Run' evangelism and the dawn of a new era of disciple-making.

Andy Considers Our EDEN Workers

Around 100 years ago, over two-thirds of the Christians in the world lived in Europe. It appears that our God who has committed himself to building his Church throughout history, and who has made it clear that he wants a people from every tribe, tongue and nation to be part of that church, wasn't satisfied with this situation. So he started to move in the hearts of his people in Europe, giving many of them, as they prayed and offered their lives to him, an incredible passion for the poor and the lost of far-off lands such as Africa, South America, India and China. This passion led to a missionary movement that has turned the world upside down. The situation now is that the vast majority of the Christians in the world live in the very lands to which these missionaries were sent.

The heroes of this movement were people like Gladys Aylward who, despite being an uneducated parlour maid, was convinced God had called her to China. She was turned down by several mission agencies before being accepted to join a 73-year-old missionary lady in Yangcheng. She set out over land with only her Bible, passport and two pounds and nine pence! After many weeks, Gladys arrived in China and proceeded to lead many Chinese nationals to the Lord. She has left an incredible legacy of Christian evangelism and good work in this vast nation.

Then there was C T Studd, who was altogether different from Gladys. He was a member of the aristocracy, a millionaire in today's terms, and captain of the England cricket team. He had it all but gave up the lot and, despite ferocious opposition and illness, returned again and again to the mission fields in India, Africa and China, often against medical advice. Even my great-grandfather Robert Hawthorne could be included in this list of 'greats'. In 1887, he left England for India on a one-way ticket. The journey took three months and when he got there, he vied with his friends to come up with different creative ideas to win the lost for Jesus. Eventually he took to wearing Indian clothes, complete with turban and no shoes, and changing his name to Jai Bai, desperately trying to become 'all things to all men to win a few.'

I find these people such a spur and a challenge to my often babyish self-centred relationship with Jesus. They were people who had caught something of God's heart and in one sense, were completely lost to this world and living for the next. At *The Message*, we are praying for similar radical disciples who will spend not three months on a boat to the heart of China but three hours or so on a train or in a car to live in the heart of the inner city on an *EDEN* project. We live in a nation where over four-fifths of the Christians live in the suburbs alongside one-fifth of the people and over four-fifths of the people live in the urban areas alongside about one-fifth of the Christians. Is it any wonder the meat is going off in these places? There simply isn't enough salt. Is it any wonder that these places are very dark when there aren't enough people letting their light shine?

It now appears that once again God is on the case of his people challenging and encouraging them to live a different way – serving the poor and the lost and moving into Manchester's most deprived communities. We now have around 150 people living long-term in Manchester's most difficult areas. Their main role is to live a godly life in these communities, praying for and serving their neighbours and having full confidence that the gospel works in any and every situation, no matter how dark. They also run discipleship groups for the increasing number of people, particularly young people, who are coming to faith and working alongside the full-time team in each project. They are working to make sure that everybody in these communities gets repeated opportunities to hear the gospel and accept or reject Jesus for themselves.

EDEN is, without a doubt, the bedrock of all we do at *The Message*. My mate Phil Wall calls it a 'tough calling and not for the faint hearted' and he's dead right but the really cool thing is that it's working. Bit by bit, we are seeing crime figures coming down and churches growing in these needy places, with the promise of so much more to come as we push on with our dream of 300 workers – Gideon's army living large in the inner city for Jesus.

The Horizontal and Vertical Cross

I want to know Christ and the power of his resurrection, and the fellowship of sharing in his sufferings, becoming like him in his death, and so, somehow, to attain resurrection from the dead. Philippians 3:10–11.

If you haven't noticed by now what this chapter, and in fact this whole book, is really saying then it is that the inner life of the evangelist is what really matters. You strangely ordinary girls and guys working out this awkward job description 'evangelist' should be living simply and contagiously to know Jesus and be like him. I've yet to be convinced that there is anything more important in the whole of human existence than becoming a trusted friend of Christ and being transformed, shade by shade, into his glory. The problem is, it's not a passive process; it doesn't just happen. You don't wake up in the morning and blind yourself in the bathroom mirror due to accidentally obtaining the Glory of the Holy Prescience halfway through a dream about flying toast. Rather, there seems to be a powerful connection between what we do for God and what we become as we do. 'Dead works' won't do you any good in this department but jacking your gifts and talents into some daily God action will have you doing that caterpillar to butterfly thing in no time.

Working with the dozens of young people who've been through *Xcelerate*, it's become plain to see that there's nothing that will actually get you changing quicker than getting involved in reaching out to this generation. Evangelism is a Primary Transformer. It's right up there on the list of things God uses to bring out the best in us. You can float about in swish meetings all day and get the best Bible teaching in the solar system but there is something different which kicks in when you're face to face with lost people. Your heart is turned inside out and Jesus becomes real in new and radical ways. As we express his love horizontally to the people he has positioned around us, it makes sense of the vertical flow of grace and mercy which we continually receive ourselves. Christ's crucifixion and his resurrection have a vital and current work in this knowing and growing process.

Buckle up for a lot of Bible in this next bit.

Resurrection Power

Have you ever read the Amplified Bible? It's a special study Bible developed in the late fifties by a team of Bible scholars. It unpacks a lot of the meaning of words and sentences which get lost between the Greek to English translation. Listen to this, from Philippians 3:10.

'For my determined purpose is that I may know him – that I may progressively

become more deeply and intimately acquainted with him, perceiving and recognising and understanding the wonders of his person more strongly and clearly. And in that same way, come to know the power outflowing from his resurrection...'

There is a dramatic focus of power and clarity of perception brought through the resurrection; it's the old 'I was blind but now I see' cliché. The power of the resurrection appeals beyond the senses, it calls to the deepest place, the hardest heart. I've heard the message of the cross preached a thousand times. Sometimes I struggle with guilty thoughts as I catch myself thinking, '...but isn't this message getting a bit tired?' yet every time, even after two thousand years, the power to salvation proves as explosive as ever.

For the apostle Paul and the churches he planted and watered, the vertical resurrection of Jesus was an ongoing revelation. Every day, Paul urged Christians to reach higher in their knowledge of the Lord. He was determined about this purpose over absolutely everything. Take his letter to the Ephesians, listen to this:

'I keep asking that the God of our Lord Jesus Christ, the glorious Father, may give you the Spirit of wisdom and revelation, so that you may know him better. I pray also that the eyes of your heart may be enlightened in order that you may know the hope to which he has called you, the riches of the glorious inheritance of the saints, and his incomparably great power for us who believe. That power is like the working of his mighty strength, which he exerted in Christ when he raised him from the dead and seated him at his right hand in the heavenly realms, far above all rule and authority, power and dominion, and every title that can be given, not only in this present age but also in the one to come.' Ephesians 1:17–21.

If we weigh it up with our logical western minds, the resurrection and ascension seem to have put not less but more distance between Jesus and the people he came to reach. *Delirious* catch the concept really well in their banging track 'Obsession' on the *Live and In the Can* album – 'Sometimes you're further than the moon, sometimes you're closer than my skin...'. I know it often feels like that in my life; one day he's right there with me, the next he can seem a million miles away. That's why I get so encouraged by Paul's prayer here. It steers my hand in my grasping for God...' bring me that Spirit of Wisdom and Revelation, God, I need to know you better.' His resurrection power enables us to know him. It's not a complicated point but it's definitely worth lingering on – if there were no resurrection we wouldn't be able to know Christ. More than that, we would not be able to enjoy loving him and feeling his love for us.

Real love belongs to the living, not the dead. It's commented on in the film *Good Will Hunting*. Matt Damon plays Will, a juvenile genius with a head full of knowledge about artists, historians, philosophers, dead people. Robin Williams begins to mentor him, to bring him into the land of the living. In one scene, they're sitting on a park bench, Robin Williams needs to find words to connect with Will at a level beyond his brilliant intellect and quietly asks,

'Have you ever woken early, gazed at your sleeping wife and thought – "God, you have put an angel on this earth just for me?"'

He's saying, look, it's not enough to know about someone, knowledge is nothing without intimacy. Christ's resurrection makes intimacy with him a reality, not just a theory. His divine love not only invades our minds but touches our emotions. The mechanics come in through a truth which Paul explains in the next chapter of his letter,

'...God raised us up with Christ and seated us with him in the heavenly realms...'

We realise that as he has been raised 'far above', so we are far above every challenge we face as we live for him. We are above every insult, every worry, every lie, every threat. Yes, they are real but they are only temporary – Jesus is real, and he is eternal. When you really catch this, it's awesome. Think about it this way – when Jesus was raised, he was able to enter a room where his disciples were meeting, even though all the doors and windows were locked. The walls were real, but in his resurrection, he was more real! What barrier can be created by the substance of the temporary to restrict the freedom of the eternal?

You can take a minute to have a KitKat and think about that, if you want!

chapter three

The Way of the Cross

Welcome back. Let's continue this amplified journey through the book of Phillipians, taking up the thread in chapter 3 at verse 10.

'...and that I may so share his sufferings as to be continually transformed in spirit into his likeness even to his death.'

The cross is a profound image of the whole Christian life because it visualises not only a vertical ascension with Christ but a horizontal journey with him, too. The cross is as much a symbol of discipleship as it is of salvation! Jesus began to teach his disciples the importance of this principle way before they could ever comprehend its full impact for them. In Luke 9 we find some intriguing dialogue... from 20, 'Who do you say I am?' – Peter answered, 'The Christ of God.'

Jesus strictly warned them not to tell this to anyone. And he said, 'The Son of Man must suffer many things and be rejected by the elders, chief priests and teachers of the law, and he must be killed and on the third day be raised to life. Then he said to them all: If anyone would come after me, he must deny himself and take up his cross daily and follow me. For whoever wants to save his life will lose it, but whoever loses his life for me will save it. What good is it for a man to gain the whole world and yet lose or forfeit his very self? If anyone is ashamed of me and my words, the Son of Man will be ashamed of him...'

Living all out for God and reaching this generation will mean rejecting the world's seductive suggestions. Any of our EDEN workers here in Manchester will tell you from personal experience that answering God's call to serve will often mean frustration and pain. Without that suffering, nobody would be able to know Christ very deeply. Of course only people who are a carrot short of a casserole go looking for suffering, but actually, it's just as daft to run away from it. Trust in God and look for the fellowship of Christ to provide the strength to overcome each difficult situation. Be determined that every difficulty you face will serve to purify you, not pollute you. Suffering will bring out the best in you or the worst in you – it's your choice.

Let's go deeper here, Jesus wasn't just being sensational to give his disciples heebie-jeebies and grab the headlines of the Galilee Gazette. His thoughts are higher than our thoughts and his ways higher than our ways; as God he always sees in the light of eternity. What's being opened here by JC is the definition and goal of discipleship. The definition of discipleship is simply 'following Jesus', the goal is to be like him.

One last time, let's turn to the trusty Amplified for the resounding echo of translation...

'If any person wills to come after me, let him deny himself – that is, disown himself, forget, lose sight of himself and his own interests, refuse and give up himself – and take up his cross daily, and follow me [that is, cleave steadfastly to me, conform wholly to my example, in living and, if need be in dying also].' Luke 9:23.

The way of the cross is the way to be like him. Sacrificial following is the way for us to attain the glorious transformation he intends for us. It's gonna involve letting go of many precious things – home, career, relationship... I even prayed a stupid prayer (not so) many years ago, 'God, even if my house gets burgled and they nick my one-of-a-kind specially imported Tommy Hilfiger puffa jacket, then not my will, but thine be done...'

A real 'Gethsemane' moment, let me tell you!

As we follow the leading of the Spirit into the company of the liars and the losers, the violent and the vulnerable, we start living a new life of fellowship with him. In another letter, this time to the church in Philippi, Paul describes this life as knowing Christ and 'and the power of his resurrection and the fellowship of sharing in his sufferings'. They are his sufferings, not ours. In his love, he allows us to share them so that we can reach our destination: to know him; and make our transformation: to be like him. It's the ultimate destiny for every extra ordinary evangelist he calls.

chapter three

body language

The 'famous Christian' syndrome is
something to laugh about, and certainly
not to take seriously. The mad joy
that comes from knowing that more
people know of your existence is a
pathetic pursuit.

Jeff Lucas

Body Language

chapter four

Take a minute to freewheel with me in your imagination. Try to picture the words that you have spoken in the past few days, your conversations, phone calls, arguments, excuses. Can you visualise them as a collective whole, taking on a life and form of their own... what would they look like? A twinkling star? A boat in a storm? An electric drill? Or maybe something more human? A child who's lost his mum? A socialite with bushy wig and fake pearls? A customer service phone rep on his 600th call?

Well, God's word did take on form, skin and bone – Jesus, the Incarnation, God's body language! Jesus became the perfect human embodiment of all that God desired to communicate to us. Before we go any further here, let's fast forward through the first page of John's Gospel.

'In the beginning was the Word, and the Word was with God, and the Word was God. He was with God in the beginning. Through him all things were made; without him nothing was made that has been made. In him was life, and that life was the light of men. The light shines in the darkness, but the darkness has not understood it... He was in the world, and though the world was made through him, the world did not recognise him. He came to that which was his own, but his own did not receive him... The Word became flesh and made his dwelling among us. We have seen his glory, the glory of the One and Only, who came from the Father, full of grace and truth.'

In a very similar way, as newborn children of God, our life, too, is a very powerful message. In fact, all our wise words and good deeds don't mean much if they aren't evident in and overflowing from our life. We are human beings, not human sayings or human doings. Look at yourself in the mirror and ask yourself this, 'What other Jesus are my friends and family likely to meet today, apart from the one looking back at me here?' What other gospel are they going to read today, other than the one they read in your life?

I spent a few years living on the *EDEN* project in Wythenshawe. We'd refer to our curious existence as 'life in the goldfish bowl'. The kids we are reaching are constantly around us and they see everything. Good and bad. Anger and peace. Division and sharing. Sometimes they tell us off! Our lives are on permanent display. The importance of our 'body language' is heightened on an 'incarnational' project like *EDEN* but the principle applies to believers everywhere. All your actions and reactions tell a story, you are the fifth gospel, the only Bible those around may have the chance to read. Don't get panicked and worried though; have peace, chill. Remember that we aren't living a pious Christian life from a dusty textbook; we are simply keeping in step with the Spirit.

Clever theologians will tell you that the Bible isn't a systematic theology, it's a history of relational theism... what? That just means the Bible tells the story of the continuous involvement of God in, through and over the lives of his creation – God interacting with people. And he's not changed his working method. First of all, he wants you to recognise your own worth in his eyes. We see this most clearly expressed in the gift of his Son to us. His death paying the price for our sins erases any doubt you might have about how precious and valuable you are to God. When we've accepted this truth and renounced our puny efforts at self-fulfilment, we're ready to start a new life of image-bearing for him. There are no entrance exams to sit, just a willingness to be used. According to your willingness, he will send you.

'Peace be with you! As the Father has sent me, I am sending you.' (John 20:21)

As we embody the message, we should draw on all our God-given intelligence and creativity to deliver the message wherever we are sent. On *Xcelerate*, in the spirit of Acts 2:14, we've found that God will work though our lives to produce a demonstration of his love and power – in life and community. In the same way that Peter stood up before the crowd in Acts 2, we will find ourselves called to explain the demonstration through a declaration, not necessarily setting up a soap box in the park, but we certainly aim to interpret the events affecting young people's lives according to what we know of God through his word.

Jesus did this; we call his interpretations 'parables', just stories and metaphors really.

One of the kids that I spent a lot of time with down in Wythenshawe was called Lee. He was a bit of a squirt and got bullied a lot when I first started spending time with him – now he's about 6' 4" and nobody gives him any grief! Every Saturday morning, he'd come round at about nine o'clock, usually with his three little brothers close behind him. They'd be bored stiff and looking for something to do. Generally I'd fill up a bucket and get the little guys washing the car while Lee and

I talked about last night's *WWF Slam Jam*. There's one particular Saturday that stands out in my memory more than the others. I'd pulled out a couple of old brushes and a tin of paint and got Lee to help me touch up the window frames. The attraction for Lee was that the task meant he could climb up the ladder and show off to his little bros from the top of the bay window. It was a really nice day for it and after a while, we sat down for a bit of a tea break – like proper council workmen. Right out of nowhere, as if he'd been lining up his moment, Lee asked me a pointed question,

'Err, Matt... what does it mean to be a Christeeeaan?'

We'd talked about God from time to time, but what that usually meant was me shoe-horning God into a conversation in a way that didn't really fit. I was pretty stunned by Lee's unsolicited curiosity. I sat back and did one of those wise-looking adult faces, curling my brow into a bit of a frown, rubbing my chin and gazing out into the ether. Inside I was in panic!

'God, help! I get a chance like this about once every six months... aaaaagh... God, don't let me blow it!'

From our vantage point up on the bay window, we could see across the little park to Lee's house. As usual, his dad had a bashed-up old car jacked up in the garden awaiting major surgery.

'You see that old Sierra your dad's got in the yard, mate?' Lee nodded.

'Well, imagine we dropped a three-litre Cozzy engine in it.'

'...sick!'

'Well, that's like becoming a Christian. God gets right inside your life, takes out the crappy way you've been living and lets you start again with some proper power.'

'Yeah! Sick, man! Wicked!'

It might not have been the most eloquent or accurate description of the glorious overcoming destiny of the redeemed but for Lee, that boring Saturday morning became a real God moment. The gospel finally reached his ears in a language he could understand.

Love Letters

Can I ask you a personal question? Have you ever been in lurve? Or are you possibly in lurve right now? I hope so; it's a great feeling and I won't be offended at all if, every once in a while, your mind wanders away from the pages of this intensely riveting book into cloudy dreamland where you skip hand in hand through sand dunes with your honey-honey.

My first love was one of the girls from Enid Blyton's *Famous Five*. She had a dog and lots of accidents. They clearly needed me to be complete as a unit – me, George the tomboy and the dog. I can't begin to tell you how utterly devastated I was when I found out that she wasn't real. I remember it vividly, as though it were yesterday, which, by the way, it wasn't. I moped around that static caravan for about three whole hours, promising myself that when I got to big school, I wasn't going to let down my defences ever again. Of course, since then, my heart's been tossed around by various floozies! But now, in case you're wondering, I'm happily married – I've found my true love... cloudy dreamland... skipping hand in hand through the sand dunes... sorry, drifted away for a minute there.

Have you ever sent a love letter – or e-mail? I've got a mate who spent two years e-mailing to and fro over the Atlantic before finally tying the knot with his sweetheart. Proper *Sleepless in Seattle* stuff. I think he kept HotMail in business single-handedly. Grace and I were a similar case. I think they categorise us as LDRs – Long Distance Relationships. It's amazing how many excuses you can come up with for 'just passing through' Glasgow at two o'clock in the morning. I know people who still keep love letters from years and years ago. It's great; the world would be so naff without love letters. Another way to look at this whole incarnational thing is to consider God's love letter to the world.

Let's take 2 Corinthians 3:3 as our starting point:

'You show that you are a letter from Christ... written not with ink but with the spirit of the living God, not on [pages of paper] but on [pages] of human hearts.'

God is love. Not too many people would argue with that as a God attribute. And Jesus, we've previously agreed was 100% God, summing up the whole message, the Word become flesh. The Father's motivation for sending his only Son into the world? *'Because God soooo loved the world...'*

What message did his Son Jesus bring?

'Love the Lord your God with all your heart and with all your soul and with all your mind.'

'Love your neighbour as yourself.'

'Love your enemies.'

Was this verbal message complemented or contradicted by the life Jesus

He will come in and
flood our lives with
love. Divine,
sacrificial, world-
changing love!

lived? You'll be searching the Scriptures for a long time to find proof of his life ever getting out of sync with his words. Jesus hated hypocrisy – in fact he invented the word! Did you know that? At the time of his life and ministry, 'hypocrites' was the word used to describe the actors who would perform from town to village in travelling shows. In the course of a theatrical event, they would play different characters, each represented by a mask, hiding the true face. Jesus hijacked the term and gave it the broader meaning we associate with it today – a person projecting an image of virtue and goodness but concealing a shady hidden side. Jesus showed that 'love' is a verb – a doing word. You've no doubt used the phrase 'fall in love'; it expresses that helpless feeling that seems to be part of the package. When we let down our defences and open the door to Jesus, he will come in and flood our lives with love. Divine, sacrificial, world-changing love!

Let's have a closer look at what Paul is trying to say in 2 Corinthians 3.

'You are a letter from Christ.'

That letter must be *important*, first class delivery, so don't hang about. When you see a need, get in there. The letter must be *legible*; can people really read you or are you just confusing the issue? When Grace and I were going out, she'd often send me letters which I'd have to read over and over again, thinking 'Well, what on earth does that mean?' Nobody should have to read between the lines in your life; make the message clear. Finally, that letter will be *precious*; nobody ever throws away a true love letter. If the love of God is shining through in your life, you shouldn't need to worry about rejection, you're more likely to be wondering, 'Where's my personal space gone? – aaaagh!'

'Written not with ink but with the Spirit.'

Ink describes some kind of human effort, an attempt to make an impression. It is ultimately temporary, destined to fade. Spirit is God, inspired and initiated. It is timeless and permanent, always bringing renewed life. We have to be full of the Holy Spirit to make any eternal effect on someone. Next time you're chatting with friends, say to yourself, 'God, give me some Spirit words to jot on these hearts.'

'On human hearts.'

To read this love letter, it's no good looking at your own heart; you must gather together the pages of other people's lives that you've had contact with, the words written there are your witness. Take a minute to imagine just that. Think about a person you've met today or earlier this week. Whether you're aware of it or not, you have made an impression on their life. I don't know if you've ever heard of the great forensic scientist, Lockhard? He developed a working method of detection which revolutionised his field. It's now known as Lockhard's principle – every contact leaves a trace.

What trace have you left behind on the lives you've touched this week? If you're worried that it might not be printable, then use the next few minutes to agree with God that from today you will only leave behind traces of Love, Hope, Encouragement, Forgiveness, Acceptance and Joy.

Love in Action

I mentioned a little while ago that love is a verb, a doing word. Let's zoom in a bit closer on that, to magnify an attribute of love which can save us from being a generation which *nearly* made it. Some of Manchester's student crowd organised a Christian event at one of the city centre nightclubs; they called it 'Dance upon Injustice'. The place was decked out with drapes, funky lighting effects and all that jazz. I noticed some groovy projections spinning around on the wall; one of them hit me like a brick:

COMPASSION: LOVE IN ACTION

What a great slogan! I want that on a T-shirt, except compassion is not a commodity; it cannot be bought or sold.

Compassion is: Love of the 'now' moment.

Compassion is: Love of the present tense.

Compassion is: Love with direction.

Compassion is: Love with focus.

The Bible talks a lot about this almost forgotten human quality. In Colossians 3:12 we are urged:

'...clothe yourselves with compassion, kindness, humility, gentleness and patience. Bear with each other and forgive whatever grievances you may have

against one another. Forgive as the Lord forgave you. And over all these virtues put on love, which binds them all together in perfect unity.'

This passage is talking about getting dressed for our daily lives as Christians. It's our casual wardrobe, what we wear for our everyday encounters with our fellow Planet Earth inhabitants. It's quite a different wardrobe from the one Paul talks about in Ephesians chapter 6, 'the armour of God'. I've heard a thousand sermons on that but next to nothing on this! And I know it can be easy to get confused; you can start thinking that the armour is for your everyday dealings with the scary people you meet in your daily life. It's not! The armour, Paul clearly instructs in Ephesians 6:12, is for battling against principalities and powers, not people! When we're hanging out with people, we slip on the pants of compassion. Yes, pants of compassion. Well, they get the first mention – what do you put on first?

Jesus wore them, discreetly, under his tunic.

'When he saw the crowds, he had compassion on them, because they were harassed and helpless, like sheep without a shepherd'. (Matt 9:36)

The apostle John expands the theme, teaching on it in 1 John 3:16–18:

'This is how we know what love is: Jesus Christ laid down his life for us. And we ought to lay down our lives for our brothers. If anyone has material possessions and sees his brother in need but has no pity on him, how can the love of God be in him? Dear children, let us not love with words or tongue but with actions and in truth.'

If you were to read that in the Amplified, you'd notice that it uses the phrase 'Closes his heart of compassion' at v17. In the good old King James, it says, 'shutteth up his bowels of compassion'. Great adjectives they had in the 16th century.

chapter four

The point is: Compassion comes from deeeep inside.
The point is: Compassion is about being *open*, not *closed*.
The point is: Compassion is about *vulnerability*, not *security*.

This is very real to our workers in Manchester, having kids knocking on the door every night of the week. They have an innate skill of arriving right in the middle of something. Often something important. The choice is either to open the door and welcome them or to close it and be ignorant. Until you've been there for some time, you really can't appreciate what a hard choice it is. The temptation to dive for cover under the sofa after a hard day can be overwhelming. The inclination to 'cop out' will always be there.

Right back in the very early days of the *EDEN* project, when I'd not been living in Wythenshawe very long, I was presented with one of these 'cop out' moments. It was a Saturday afternoon which had begun to stretch on into early evening. Everything was so new that those of us who'd taken up the challenge to move into the area were still in the awkward process of trying to suss each other out. We'd just ordered a bunch of tickets for *Titanic*, which was breaking all the '90s box office records. As we sat around chatting, there was a knock at the door. Everything went quiet, in the way that kids do when you walk in on them doing something naughty. I shrugged with a puzzled 'I dunno' expression my face and got up to answer the door.

On the doorstep stood a girl I instantly recognised; she was one of the older sisters in a large and notorious local family. She was at a loose end so I stepped out and began to chat on the path with her. Her younger brother, a lad known to us all as being responsible for about 90% of the crime on the estate, had been arrested. I knew full well that since we'd moved into the street, he'd already burgled my friend's house twice, as well as vandalising our cars and hurling abuse at us. So he'd been arrested. Oh, and he was stuck in a police cell on the other side of Manchester? Hard luck. Thing was, God wouldn't allow me to think like that. He prodded me and I had to do something about it.

I agreed there and then to take the girl, along with one of the female members of our team, to go and sort out his release. It became one of the biggest breakthroughs we had. Of course, when we'd prayed for breakthroughs this wasn't exactly what we'd had in mind but God knew what he was doing. We stepped out of our routine. We took a risk. We paid a price, not a big one, a gallon of petrol and a couple of tickets to *Titanic*. In return, we shared something very special with the kids we've been reaching out to. It became the foundation of a really quality relationship. Keith Green sings a song with some challenging lyrics:

> *'Jesus rose from the dead, you can't even get out of bed...*
> *Jesus came to your door, you've left him out on the street.'* Gets me every time.

Can you recall any times this week when you've opened your heart to someone?

Can you recall any times this week when you've closed it? It's simple 'Good Samaritan' stuff, not quantum discipleship for the super-holy. Compassion can be the key.

'BIG UP' your Compassion

As we follow the heartbeat of Jesus towards the lost and the broken, we'll need to square up to all sorts of challenges, some external, but many internal. There are strengths and weaknesses in our lives which can be either bridges or barriers to the expression of compassion.

chapter four

BRIDGES	BARRIERS
Relationship	Prejudice
Honesty	Hypocrisy
Availability	Busyness
Humility	Pride
Risks	Comfort

The table really speaks for itself. However, we'll spend just a few pages now touching on some of these factors in a bit more detail.

Pride and Prejudice (and Busyness)

Looking back on the time before I became a Christian, I recognise that I had a problem with people of other races. I wasn't a member of the National Front or anything like that but I had a very generalised and narrow-minded view of cultures alien to me. I'd grown up in an environment with very little ethnic diversity and the little contact which I'd had only served to reinforce my stereotypes. This was a problem which greatly affected my level of compassion. The poor and needy were simply outside my demographic. It's far easier to dismiss a cry for help when no framework of empathy exists. God dealt with this area in a very straightforward way. Almost without my noticing, he led me into experiences and relationships which broke down my misconceptions and enriched my character.

Ten years on and I'm even in a mixed-race marriage. It's the most normal thing in the world once God's opened your eyes.

A very real pressure and possibly the most frequent and even plausible excuse for actually getting away with doing nothing is 'busyness'. The universal scourge of the church and of Christian ministry, it comes in various strains, most commonly, 'meetingitis'. Paul Harris from the Evangelical Alliance popped to *Xcelerate* recently. He left us with this enduring thought:

'Meetings eat people.' Think about it.

A few Januarys ago, I made the New Year resolution not to be 'busy', and I tried hard to eradicate the word from my vocabulary. But instead, I found myself having 'commitments', or being 'proactive' in lots of areas. It's a constant pressure for anyone in any kind of ministry; many of you might be entering this sort of realm, too. The only way out is to question your priorities, regularly. In fact, I'd go further than that, I'd say, *constantly*. Be ruthless and learn to say 'NO', even to things which are good, valuable and enjoyable. I could easily fill my week with two or three management meetings a night and never actually do what God has called me to do, which is to get alongside the young people who don't know Jesus. It's become a personal stake in the ground for me. I will not go a week without spending some time simply hanging out with kids who need God.

How about you? What has God called you to do and have you weighed it in the balance opposite your other commitments? Sometimes you have to sacrifice the good to get the best. That's often described as the difference between the permissible and the perfect will of God.

Hand in hand with busyness walks pride. We can get our heads stuck so far in our (to quote the King James again) bowels, with self importance – 'I'm the Executive Director of chair-stacking' – that our compassion level dwindles to zero. Compassion is outward-looking and you can't look outwards if you're always looking at yourself. Don't let it happen. God made us all with a great capacity for love and compassion and he will lead us into areas of opportunity. Our decision is to *open*, to let it happen. Reorganise and reprioritise and step into that area of action and truth, rather than words or tongue. If you recognise you need to do that, then put this book down and pray about it right away.

Expression of Compassion

Smith Wigglesworth is a man shrouded in Pentecostal legend. I imagine that God usually really enjoyed but sometimes had to endure his antics,

'Oh, Smith – clean your ears out – I said kiss the baby, now look what you've done!'

Not a lot of people are aware of it but Smith started his ministry on the docks in Liverpool. He felt God moving his heart, drawing him to a bunch of scally kids; their dads were generally out at sea, their mums generally down the gin shop. He worked all the hours he could as a plumber and spent every penny that he earned feeding the little urchins. No preaching. No healings. Just raw compassion. Eventually, he felt God leading him back to Bradford where he got married and where most of the 'ministry' reports begin. I'd like to suggest that he was only ready for that miracle ministry after God had laid the deep foundations of compassion in his soul.

Here he speaks of how that deep compassion turned him into a great preacher, with a bit of help from his wife:

'My wife was a great preacher, and although I had no ability to preach, she made up her mind to train me for the ministry. So she would continually make an announcement that I would be the speaker the next Sunday. She said she was sure I could preach if I only tried. When she announced me to speak, this would give me a week of labour and a good deal of sweating. I used to go into the pulpit on Sunday with great boldness, give out my text, say a few words, and then say to the congregation, "If any of you can preach, you can have a chance now, for I am finished."

'She would have me try again but it always ended the same way. She was the preacher and I encouraged her to do it all. But I found out that when you have a burden for lost souls, and the vision of their need is ever before you, the Lord, as you look to Him, will give you expression to your heart's compassion and make a preacher out of you. We held open-air services for twenty years in one part of the city of Bradford. It was as I ministered in the open-air week by week that the Lord began to give me more liberty.'

What a great phrase, *'the Lord, as you look to Him, will give you expression to your heart's compassion.'*

Maybe, like me, you can think of times in your life when you've had compassion, but felt utterly helpless to do anything with it. Compassion without expression. I have vivid memories of standing in a park in the rain at the end of a summer mission. The rest of the team had packed up the gear and zoomed off in their cars. Two little boys were looking up at me silently with big dewy eyes. I'd become aware of their awful circumstances during that week and my heart was breaking. I did not have a clue what to do. I desperately needed some expression but at that time, none came. We just got wet together.

The other side of the equation is when expression exists without compassion. Classic open-air scenario. When I first joined my church, I found myself involved in lots of this. Bloke stands in public square with guitar and knitted jumper. Small crowd of people gather around, pretending to be the general public. The stupid, the gullible and the over-keen, me fitting the bill perfectly, distribute literature to passers-by in vain hope of getting a few words of conversation. In all fairness, though, for most of us, there was merely a sense of duty with the compassionometer barely showing any signs of life.

For effective people-reaching, we totally need both compassion and expression. The tandem effect takes interpersonal contact to a whole different level. Ministry becomes truly relational. To pinch a phrase from business, it's a value added moment.

When my final year at Uni was drawing to a close, I began planning the next steps. I was keen to travel the world, especially if I could serve God at the same time. An idea of sheer brilliance hit me. I would take a final student loan and book a ticket to Australia. Never mind about the five years it would take me to pay it back, I would be alone with the Lord and he would show me his will for the next fifty years of my life. Genius! Even though it's hard to believe now that I was once so random, God did meet me and bless me on that trip. Travelling through Queensland, I would get up early and go down to the beach to read the Word and worship God. The privilege of sharing his company at that time was overwhelming. However, one morning I discovered that I wasn't alone. Two lads were also loitering with intent on the beach. They came over and introduced themselves, just as I was packing my stuff away.

'Do you believe that there can be heaven on earth?' the older of the two asked me.

'Funny you should ask...' I replied.

Quick as a flash, the leaflets were out, colourful illustrations of smartly dressed families sitting in glorious landscapes with their nicely brushed hair blowing gently in the unpolluted breeze. Lions and lambs were playing in the grass. My heart went out to the two lads. The younger one was clearly scared stiff and his mate wasn't looking all that confident either. I wasn't about to launch into fierce theological debate with them. I also reckoned that even a 12-year-old Jehovah's Witness probably knew more about the Bible than I did at that stage. Instead I invited them to sit down with me as I felt the Holy Spirit giving me expression to what was in my heart for them. For the next fifteen or twenty minutes, I was able to explain to them what I'd been doing down there on the beach. I had liberty to share with them the intimacy of my relationship with Jesus. I overstepped the mark a bit by offering to pray with them and they decided to make a move. The impression was made, though, and the seed was planted. God had caused compassion and expression to combine to his glory. It can happen at the most unexpected moment.

That experience on the beach was a great God 'accident'. Bring 'em on, Lord! It showed me that wherever I am, I can be incarnational and relational. Look at the ministry of Jesus; he was relational, even if only for two minutes. Later in the book, we'll be looking at what it takes to go all the way but for goodness sake, don't not be involved in reaching out to people just because you aren't sure where the next link in the chain is coming from. *Xcelerate* is only a five-month course and we have to put right that attitude from the outset. God can do amazing, significant and eternal things in five months. In fact, he shows time and again that he can turn lives around in five minutes.

As we wrap up this chapter, which has covered quite a wide horizon of material, particularly the challenge of embodying love and compassion, I'd like to give the final word to the apostle Paul:

'The only thing that counts is faith expressing itself through love.' (Gal 5:6)

chapter
four

chapter five

the gospel manifesto

Sin is not a measure of how bad you are but it is a measure of how good you are not.

Life Manifesto

What is this news that is so urgent for us evangelists to communicate? Who's it for... and how do we find them? If we do find ourselves with a God opportunity to pass on this great news, how on earth do we expect people to respond to it? Peter found himself in that situation in Acts 2. I don't think he was up late the night before prepping his message, and nobody had ever posed the question to him, 'What have I got to do to be saved?' The answer was alive inside him:

'Repent and be baptised, every one of you, in the name of Jesus Christ, for the forgiveness of your sins. And you will receive the gift of the Holy Spirit. The promise is for you and your children and for all who are far off – for all whom the Lord our God will call.'

Everything Peter tried to be, say and do was inspired by the time he'd spent with the main man. Jesus had taken him from being a foul-mouthed fisherman to being an on-the-ball people-reacher. What would Peter have picked up hanging around with the Christ? To answer that question, I've invited Ness Wilson, who looks after a radical university campus church in the Midlands. Ness regularly jumps on the train to come and have some input with our *Xcelerators*. She unpacks for us here the ministry of Jesus which Peter, together with the other eleven, would have witnessed and participated in.

We're going to start in Luke 4, where we see the launch of Jesus' ministry in a powerful and prophetic declaration which sums up his life manifesto:

'The Spirit of the Lord is on me, because he has anointed me to preach good news to the poor. He has sent me to proclaim freedom for the prisoners and recovery of sight for the blind. To release the oppressed. To proclaim the year of the Lord's favour.'

In order to understand the context of why he was declaring such powerful words in the middle of a normal synagogue service, we need to understand something of the background of the synagogue. It was the centre of spiritual life in Palestine. The Law said that wherever there were ten Jewish families, there must be a synagogue in which the people could meet to worship. No sacrifices were made in the synagogue – that was for the temple only. The synagogue was for worship and teaching. A typical synagogue service was divided into three parts:

Worship – where prayers were offered up to God.

Reading out loud of scripture – seven people from the congregation would read.

Teaching – this was not undertaken by any professional ministry. It was simply open for anyone with a message or thoughts to share, then it would all be discussed. Quite a challenge for our models of church and professional ministry that take place today!

This, then, is how Jesus, a local carpenter, was given access to speak. Jesus was one of the readers and was simply handed the scroll that contained Isaiah 61 so he read it out. As he read, says the Bible, *'the eyes of everyone in the synagogue were fastened on him'*, which gives us the picture of the authority and power with which he read these incredible words. People would have been familiar with hearing this passage but this time, it was different. As Jesus read it out, there was a growing sense of awe and wonder within the congregation as they realised the way in which Jesus was owning these words.

After reading the passage, it says, 'he rolled up the scroll, gave it back to the attendant and sat down.' We often view this statement through our cultural lenses and assume that means he was finished. Not so! In fact it means he was just about to start – the speaker in a synagogue gave talks sitting down. He begins to unpack the passage with these words:

'Today, this scripture is fulfilled in your hearing.'

What a statement! This local village man, who grew up as a boy amongst them, was suddenly making extraordinary claims. Not only that, he began to indicate that God's salvation plan was to include Gentiles in his mission, quoting Old Testament examples of people God responded to who were outside the Jewish nation: the widow in Zarephath and Naaman the Syrian.

Jesus was taking this passage to be his life manifesto, a declaration of what he was about, his mission on this earth. Here was a man who knew his identity, his purpose and therefore his priorities. These few verses summed him up – he was anointed by God to push back the kingdom of darkness and usher in the kingdom of light. He would bring the goodness and reality of heaven to earth, especially to the poor and the oppressed. This was the commencement of his public ministry. As the next three years unfold, we see, throughout the pages of scripture, the fulfilment of this manifesto. Wherever Jesus went he 'preached good news', mostly to the poor and to the ordinary people of the day – the non-religious, without wealth or status, and they connected with him. Wherever Jesus went, there were crowds – Jesus loved people and they loved him. The poor and marginalised seemed especially drawn to him, probably responding to the love and worth he gave to them. Most of them would never have experienced being treated like that before.

Jesus was all about 'freedom for the prisoners', those bound up and trapped by the schemes of the enemy. He broke the power of everything that robs people of living as redeemed humanity – fear, shame, guilt, addiction, all these things and more, so that people did not have to stay prisoners to them. He was about 'recovery of sight for the blind'; he saw blind eyes opened physically and saw many receive spiritual sight and revelation about who he really was.

Jesus 'released the oppressed' in all kinds of ways. He seemed particularly drawn to the victims of life, like the prostitutes and the lepers. Jesus wanted to bring healing spiritually through the forgiveness of sins but also healing emotionally through giving people dignity and value, like when he healed the leper in Luke 5:12,13. This man would have been devoid of human touch for years but Jesus deliberately touched him. The compassionate gesture of a Rabbi reaching out and tenderly placing a hand on a ravaged and disfigured body would have been a source of tremendous healing on the inside of the man, as well as the obvious external healing he received through Jesus.

Jesus also seemed to have a special love for women, who in that day and age were very much oppressed and looked down upon. He allowed women to be part of the wider group of disciples, travelling with him and learning from him (Luke 8:1–3, Luke 10:39), he used women as examples in his teaching (Luke 21:1–4) and restored the dignity of women wherever he could. Check out the woman caught in adultery (John 8:1-11). At the end of Jesus' life, it was the group of women disciples who followed him to the very end and were there at the crucifixion when all the men had fled. It was to women that Jesus chose to reveal the incredible miracle of the resurrection and it was Mary Magdalene whom he charged with the task of being the ambassador of the full gospel to the other male disciples (John 20:17–18). Here we see, even at the end of his ministry on earth, Jesus working out his gospel manifesto to 'release the oppressed', sending a woman, an ex-prostitute, to 'preach good news' and to 'proclaim the year of the Lord's favour'.

The Friendship and the Fear

So we see who his message was specifically targeted towards and we've caught the heartbeat of the content, but what do we do with it now? How far do we go with this truth we hold? As you might expect, I say, all the way. Don't fall into the trap of putting so much emphasis on one aspect of the gospel, for instance, emphasis on grace at the expense of another aspect such as repentance. It happens, and it's a real problem in evangelism today. In our desperate attempts to win people over, we leave out the 'tough bits'. We're happy to tell people that they'll have a good life and prosper, but omit to reveal that there may well be times of persecution and 'sharing in his sufferings'. We so want to project the image of 'Jesus, your best friend' that we leave out the small detail that he is also sovereign king of the universe and expects his people to submit to his authority over every aspect of their lives.

I think that one of the trickiest tasks of the process of evangelism is opening up and bringing light to the whole concept of 'Jesus is Lord'. I'm still searching on this one. The examples I have are so limited. Not many of the young people I work with have any idea what a Lord is! And if they do, they're likely to have about as much respect for him as they do for their parents, teachers, police… but this is God! If only I could just wander round and summon random visions on people of the kind Ezekiel saw, it would be fine; everybody would be believing in no time.

'…High above on the throne was a figure like that of a man. I saw that, from what appeared to be his waist up, he looked like glowing metal, as if full of fire; and brilliant light surrounded him. Like the appearance of a rainbow in the clouds on a rainy day, so was the radiance around him. This was the appearance of the likeness of the glory of the Lord. When I saw it I fell face down…'

But I've not heard of many people being reached that way, I think that for some bizarre reason God lets us struggle a bit. Of course we don't like hard work so we all too often take the easy option – yes, my hands are up – I've done it, fallen into the slippery trap of projecting to young people the idea of a neatly packaged, sanitised Jesus who wants to be your pop star/puppy/Buzz Lightyear.

Who is that helping? Let's get real. I've already said that evangelism is a primary transformer, that the more we seek to affect the lost, the more we see ourselves being changed. Flowing with this, as we're clearly in the people business, we should be the most sensitive and flexible people on the face of the earth. Is that true? Go get your dictionary... evangelist... are any of these words mentioned: patient, good listener, reserves judgement? I doubt it, yet we really should be listening, paying attention, discerning what revelation the Holy Spirit has already brought to someone before we begin our work moving them on.

I want to major on this point now. I think this is one of the major issues facing evangelists today, especially youth evangelists. We know the gospel facts. We relate to kids and youth. But we need a new anointing, enabling, courage and perseverance as we guide people to the place where they acknowledge and declare 'Jesus is Boss'.

Repentance

chapter five

In our presentation of the gospel, let's not oversimplify too much. I, for one, don't want to lose the mystery of Christ.

We have a responsibility to present God's word with integrity. Paul tells Timothy that he should '...correctly handle the word of truth...' It's an awesome, mind-stretching, soul-stretching responsibility. There are so many distractions, human frameworks of conditioning to shake off – culture, gender, politics, race and class. The common way for evangelicals is to think of a good point, then try to prove it with a string of scripture references. Quite a legal, logical, technical approach to God's word. Unfortunately, you can prove pretty much anything in that way – that's why it's the preferred method which most cults use, taking a little bit then stretching it out of all proportion. God's really not got a point to prove to you; he works on a much higher level that that. He has a purpose to reveal to you – that's far more liberating. I heard someone say recently, 'God made man in his image and we returned the favour!' In our presentation of the gospel, let's not oversimplify too much. I, for one, don't want to lose the mystery of Christ. His personality is beyond expression; his behaviour doesn't fit into any of our little human boxes. He's God and I want him to stay that way. The Holy Spirit is the convictor of sin and the revealer of God. If we simply communicate to human minds, we've failed miserably. The word of God can penetrate soul and spirit, judge the thoughts and attitudes of the heart. It opens the door to salvation, the door of repentance.

So what is repentance? It's a massively overlooked aspect of God's salvation plan which we need to get to grips with again. It's a wonderful Godly concept with a bad image problem. It's not up there in the top ten favourite topics shared with not-yet believers. However, its partner is. Scripture often uses repentance in stereo with another much more user-friendly word, forgiveness.

'And so John came, baptising in the desert region, preaching a baptism of repentance for the forgiveness of sins (Mark 1:4).

'He told them, "This is what is written: The Christ will suffer and rise from the dead on the third day, and repentance and forgiveness of sins will be preached in his name to all nations, beginning at Jerusalem. You are witnesses of these things."' Luke 24:46-48

I'd like to look at three short passages as we get into this. Read them carefully and try to catch the links as they develop.

The Journey

The first account is of troubled prophet Elijah, the Tishbite. Sounds a bit like a Palestinian mosquito wound, doesn't it? Aaaagh, I've got a Tish-bite, quick, get the TCP! Anyway, you'll find the story in 1 Kings 19:1–18.

Elijah has 'preacher's hangover' – the day after the day before. You might be able to relate to him; I certainly can. Often the most severe crisis of faith and times of temptation come right after an awesome experience of God. We find Elijah feeling scared and lonely, displaced and doubting, and once again, homeless and hungry. He prays a suicidal prayer; the words he uses are quite bizarre. He prays, 'I have had enough, LORD, take my life; I am no better than my ancestors (Verse 4).

'I'm no better than my ancestors,' he says. Not, 'I've had enough, the psycho queen is trying to kill me!' He wants to die because he feels like a waste of space. He feels unwanted. So who were these ancestors, these Tishbites, that he's got such a complex about? They were a clan of settlers living in Gilead, east of the Jordan. Historically, they were refugees; they feuded with the tribes around them and became the subject of jibes and taunts.

'You Gileadites are fugitives from Ephraim and Manasseh...' (Judg 12:4).

The harsh words lingered through the generations. Elijah had tried to shake them off; he'd tried to live differently and to please God but it seemed that his fate was sealed.

Here he was, the amazing wonder-worker, enemy of the state, on the run again, on his knees again. He was right where God wanted him. In the wisdom of God's purpose is continually expressed the will not simply to work through you, but also to work in you. Elijah was about to find this out in a very personal way. He was going to have to repent of holding on to baggage that didn't belong in the heart of God's man of the moment. The pain needed to be released – God wanted to take it away, to minister, and as usual, he wasn't going to rush the process. 'Do not forget this one thing, dear friends: with the Lord, a day is like a thousand years and a thousand years are like a day. The Lord is not slow in keeping his promise, as some understand slowness. He is patient with you, not wanting anyone to perish, but everyone to come to repentance.' (2 Pet 3:8,9)

As the story unfolds, we see God's grace expressed to Elijah. There's an angelic delivery of breakfast and lunch. There's a pilgrimage to the Sinai mountain, a trek of two hundred miles south and four hundred years back in time. On the mountain, Elijah's history will be rewritten; the ancestor complex won't bother him again after this encounter. By the time he arrives in the cave, he's ready for some dialogue with God; forty days in the desert rehearsing his speech, he's got it locked down. The Lord doesn't mince his words either:

'What are you doing here, Elijah?'

With that, the prophet is off into his tightly-scripted patter:

'I have been very zealous for the LORD God Almighty. The Israelites have rejected your covenant, broken down your altars, and put your prophets to death with the sword. I am the only one left, and now they are trying to kill me too.'

Only at this point does God begin to turn on the power. A whole forty days later. Elijah had known the great God who could stop the rain and pour down fire. He just needed to surrender himself again to the whispering God who cared about the integrity of his inner life.

We can learn a very special lesson from this, too. God shows here that he is happy to journey with us, bringing us safely to the place of revelation and submission to his will.

The Point

Secondly, turn to John 8:1,11, the woman caught in adultery. Here we are introduced to her dramatically as she was confronted face to face with her sin, accused by the mob, with no way out. Vicious, condemning voices surrounded her. She was trapped, time had run out. It was the point of no return. An inevitable point. Yes, she was sorry, she probably wailed and screamed for mercy all the way to the temple courts – but let's not feel too sorry for her. She was no angel; she'd been caught sleeping with another woman's husband. She was guilty and she knew it. But she found Jesus there. Isn't he great at that 'right place, right time' thing? He's always there, because we all become trapped by our sins; even the most secret ones have the habit of becoming public news. Ask Michael Barrymore or Naomi Campbell.

What did Jesus write in the dust? A list of sins? Scriptures or prophecy of God's mercy? As the angry gang became quiet and one by one sloped away, Jesus looked at her and spoke. His words at this crucial turning point give insight into what repentance is all about: *'Go now and leave your LIFE of sin'*.

In verse 4, the mob condemned the act. Jesus looked high and beyond. He cared for the life. The former was destroying the latter. Equipped with that revelation, the woman was ready to start again. Learn from Jesus, for yourself and for the lives of those he leads you to; the point of repentance is so much more than confessing an act of sin. It is the choice of a totally different way of life.

Products

Thirdly, I'd like to look at that awesome moment in Acts 16:22–34, the moment when hymn-singing heroes Paul and Silas found themselves at the epicentre of God's plan for the town of Philippi. The jailer is our focus. Let's try to figure out what God was doing in his life through this moment of chaos and catastrophe.

There's a widespread idea, which springs from this 'pick a verse here and a verse there' understanding of the Bible, that just believing is enough. This is the classic passage to back that up because it contains the verse 31, 'Believe in the Lord Jesus, and you will be saved – you and your household.' That's clearly not the whole story, though, is it? This piece is not just about belief. I know that's controversial but I'm not going to argue with you about it here. If you want more about that, read some of the stuff that David Wilkerson has published in the last few years. Look again; look at the drama of the whole situation. The guy was on the verge of suicide. We just talked about a woman who reached the point of repentance. He was really at the sharp end of that point.

'The jailer called for lights, rushed in and fell trembling before Paul and Silas. He then brought them out and asked, "Sirs, what must I do to be saved?"'

The jailer knew that the buck stopped with him, and consider this – his personal responsibility to earthly authorities for the lives of Paul and Silas led him to a revelation of his personal responsibility to a heavenly authority for his own life. Do you see it?

'Then they spoke the word of the Lord to him and to all the others in his house.' In comes the spirit of kindness again. I can feel the wrath there, glowing through the page. As demonstrated in the previous examples, harsh judgement only breeds harsh, judgemental people, but generous kindness breeds kind, generous people. That's the product. Look how it's revealed here:

'At that hour of the night, the jailer took them and washed their wounds… The jailer brought them into his house and set a meal before them; he was filled with joy…' (verses 33,34).

John, whose baptism ministry we mentioned at the start of this study, had this truth pinned down; he even warned those he baptised, 'produce fruit in keeping with repentance.'

'…God's kindness leads us to repentance…' (Rom 2:4).

chapter five

So Why Don't We Repent?

Pretty universally, there are three reasons. It's nothing new to try to avoid the consequences of sin; it's as old as the human race. In fact, all three reasons are contained in the first few pages of your Bible.

One, we want to hide. See Genesis 3:8. Adam and Eve in the Garden of Eden knew they had done wrong. Sin had come to them as often it does, in the heat of the moment. Impulsive foolishness... D'OH! The Lord comes looking in the cool of the day. The hopeless human reaction is to run away, or to try and cover up in some really hopeless fig-leaf kind of way. How ridiculous they must have looked. I really don't know what would've happened to the human race if they had taken a different action following their sin, if they'd gone straight to God and pleaded for mercy. We just can't say. What we can do is learn the lesson.

Two, we blame. Genesis 3:12,13. Here Adam and Eve take it out on one another and on the snake. Adam had been given ultimate responsibility. Sadly, he discredited men for ever and reduced his position when he blamed his wife. She had the opportunity to redeem the situation by accepting her role in the disaster but she blamed the serpent. Making excuses never helped anyone. My old boss used to say 'I don't want excuses, I want results!' and he got them. You must have noticed that 'blame culture' is out of control in our present world. 'Where there's blame, there's a claim!' Don't get sucked in by it. God doesn't accept excuses.

Three, we deny it. See Genesis 4:9. Cain is questioned by God after murdering his brother –'Where is your brother?' 'I don't know.'

I remember a line I heard from one shady soap opera character to another; I think it might have been Steve Owen to Billy Mitchell.

'Never underestimate the power of bare-faced denial.' Well, that might work on the residents of Albert Square but it won't work on God. Lying to God brought Cain this curse, 'You will be a restless wanderer on the earth' (verse 12). It's the same curse which falls on anyone who denies his guilt before God. Life will become an uncomfortable, directionless struggle. For many years, my own life was lived under that same restless, wandering curse. Almost every day, I see people around me still caught by it, stubbornly refusing to admit their guilt before God.

When God came alongside me at the age of twenty, after I'd spent six long years trying to avoid him, the first thing he did was to give me strength and hope for the journey. It took me a good six months to move from that unique encounter to the point of complete surrender. God made sure that I was ready to give my all. It was a Sunday night and followed one of the most roller-coaster weeks of my life. I'd just turned twenty-one. Without any appreciation of church protocol, I walked in late and looked around. I spotted a particularly holy-looking bloke; the shine on his bald head produced a halo-type effect. Without any messing about, I marched up to him and announced, *'I want to give my life to Jesus right now, all of it.'* Then I burst into tears and didn't stop for about a month!

In no time, I began feeling the desire to bless people. I'd root through my wardrobe and my drawers – shirts, jeans, trainers, what did I need all these clothes for? There were so many people around me in need. God caused a product of repentance in my life in the form of random acts of kindness, which really bore no resemblance to the selfish old me at all. From every angle, I considered myself a receiver of God's extravagant kindness; it simply had to overflow.

Think about it again – repentance, the Godly concept with an image problem. Have you given it the right position in your gospel manifesto? *'God's kindness leads us to repentance.'* (Rom 2:4)

The Fulness of Grace

What is 'grace'? It's a funny kind of word. We use it a lot, yet most of us haven't got a clue what it really is. Speaking for myself, I know I used to have a big misconception in this area. Many of our *Xcelerators* turn up with exactly the same mindset. Seemingly in the form of evangelism and discipleship commonly experienced by this generation, there is little understanding of the idea, 'I am saved – I am being saved – I will be saved.' To describe the problem more plainly, grace is all too often used as a washing powder; we get it out every time we sin, expecting it to wash the stains away. Great. We know it does, but let me ask you this. If the only purpose of grace is to be used on the sin in our lives, why did Jesus have so much of it? I don't think any of you would like to argue that he needed it to sort out his sin.

Luke 2:40 says, *'And the child grew and became strong; he was filled with wisdom, and the grace of God was upon him.'*

John backs him up in 1:14 of his Gospel:

'The word became flesh and made his dwelling among us. We have seen his glory, the glory of the only begotten, who came from the Father, full of grace and truth.'

He continues in verse 16, *'from the fullness of his grace we have received one blessing after another, for the law was given by Moses; grace and truth came by*

Jesus Christ.'

Fairly straightforward so far. Jesus led a pure and blameless life, yet demonstrated a life chokka with grace. The preconception of our minds is what prevents many from handling this. You see contrary to popular belief, grace was not designed as a cure but as a prevention. It is a gift, given to us by Christ for the enabling of a righteous life. Jesus spoke through the prophet Zechariah: *'...I will pour out on the house of David and the inhabitants of Jerusalem the Spirit of grace and supplication. They will look on me, the one they have pierced..."* (Zech 12:10)

Are you beginning to see how important grace was to Christ? Let's take a look at the importance of the work of grace in the early church. The accounts we are given in the Acts of the Apostles show just how they lived with it and through it. Starting with Acts 4:33, *'With great power, the apostles continued to testify to the resurrection of the Lord Jesus and much* (The King James has 'great') *grace was upon them all. There were no needy persons among them.'*

On an individual level, we hear of Stephen (Acts 6:8–10). *'Now Stephen, a man full of God's grace and power, did great wonders and miraculous signs among the people... they could not stand up against his wisdom of the Spirit by whom he spoke.'*

Because of persecution, particularly the high profile murder of this guy Stephen, many believers had no choice but to look further afield to live. Some felt led to go to the Greeks at Antioch. They carried with them their early church values of community. They were full of the Holy Spirit and regularly preached to the locals. A great number believed, so many that news reached Jerusalem. An envoy called Barnabas was sent to them. Many comments could have been recorded about this new church in Antioch. It was a top place – just think, this is the first place that the disciples became known as Christians. I call that significant. Interesting, then, that instead of every story and miracle the writer of the Acts could have included, this one remark was chosen, *'He [Barnabas] saw the evidence of the grace of God; he was glad and encouraged them to remain true to God with all their hearts.'* (Acts 11:23)

Note here – 'remain true'. It would be impossible for the church to remain true unless it already held an unswerving dedication to God. This was a characteristic most certainly held by Barnabas and his soon-to-be travelling companion, Paul. The two of them got together and began a journey through a wide area of what is now Turkey, as they went '...*urging people to continue in the grace of God*' (Acts 13:43). Eventually they came full circle and ended up back in Antioch again '*where they had been committed to the grace of God for the work they had now completed*' (Acts 14:26).

Before leaving these early church examples, there is one more thing worth our attention, a situation which arose and threatened to split the young church into two. The issue was circumcision for Gentile converts. Peter gave the uncompromising answer. Have a look at the reason; it's saved us fellas from a lot of pain.

'*No! We believe it is through the grace of our Lord Jesus that we [Jews] are saved, just as they [Gentiles] are*' (Acts 15:11).

The previous quotation bears the focus as we press further into this study of grace. It speaks of salvation, another concept which we can all too easily misrepresent. How many times have you looked back and said, 'I was saved on such-and-such a date'? Yes, you were, but words can trip us up; they have a great effect over the way we think. At their worst, words and ways of saying things can block the continuing path of salvation. Yes, you were saved on such-and-such a date, therefore you are present tense, saved, not were, past tense. Don't think I'm just splitting hairs here, I simply want you to grasp the continuing, fluid nature of grace which allows you to *remain* saved. Look back at Acts 11:22, 13:43 and 14:26; they all mention grace in the context of a *progress* word: 'remain'... 'continue'... 'committed'... This is a perpetual enabling of grace by which we are saved.

I can't end this lesson without dealing with some of the more disquieting aspects of grace. It would be wrong simply to preach about all the good stuff. There are dangers involved for those who refuse the biblical application of grace. My first picture described grace as a washing powder; another metaphor which describes very clearly the way grace can be abused is the illustration of the Monopoly 'Get out of Jail Free' card. I'm sure this doesn't need too much explanation. There's a great temptation to fall into sin, both unwittingly and deliberately, then simply wave the card saying, 'I believe that Jesus died for my sin. Hallelujah for his wonderful grace!'

Jonah knew the consequence of disobeying God; his life was spared that he might testify this to us in chapter 2:8 of his book:

'*Those who cling to worthless idols forfeit the grace that could be theirs. But*

I, with a song of thanksgiving, will sacrifice to you. What I have vowed, I will make good.'

Sadly, there are loads of believers out there who are risking their reward on judgement day because they put worldly things before God. In the biblical sense, that's known as 'idolatry'. That's all an idol is. It doesn't have to be a statue. Anything which dominates your life to the extent that God is pushed into second place is an idol. Tough stuff, I know. If you think these are the only tough words on the subject, think again. Hebrews 10:29 uses a phrase that should ring in our ears, '...who has insulted the Spirit of grace?'.

Deadly silence. You don't hear that very much around Sunday morning tea and biscuits. Who in his right mind would want to grieve the Holy Spirit deliberately? And after all, as Christians, we believe that he has actually taken up residence within us. I hope that you'll do all that you can to make him happy, not drive him mad!

Let's summarise a bit and recap on some of those verses we've covered. If you were paying close attention to the construction of the references, particularly the ones chosen from Acts, you'll have noticed this:

- They all mention grace – of course they do; that's the subject.
- Involved with them is a *progress word*. You know that – we've already discussed it.
- Many of them incorporate what I can only describe as a demonstration word, for want of a better one. Words such as:

  power, truth, wonders, wisdom, miraculous signs, all accompanying the outworking of a life of grace. I'd go further than that; I'd say that the *inworking* of grace produces an *outworking* of Christ. We don't need to know the deep existential theology of how this happens; we just have to believe it and apply it. There is no shortage, Ephesians 1:7–8 tells us:

  '[God] to the praise of his glorious grace, which he has given us in the one he loves [Jesus]. In him we have redemption through his blood, the forgiveness of sins in accordance with the riches of God's grace which he has lavished upon us with all wisdom and understanding.'

Grace, demonstrated by Christ's death and empowered by his resurrection. Grace by which we *are* saved, day by day a powerful testimony of God's love. Please don't try to box, shelve or package God's amazing grace and don't save it as a 'Get out of Jail Free' card. Grace is the essence, the substance, the core and the heart, the very instrument of our freedom in Christ.

chapter five

Ness began this chapter explaining the mission statement of Jesus Christ, people-centred directives we should aim for every day of our lives. We've seen how those headlines are fully qualified and achieved in human lives, though repentance, through the acceptance of Christ's Lordship, and through the beautiful gift of grace. As evangelists, our hearts beat to see people saved from sin for a holy life to eternal glory. Let's not accept anything less.

chapter six

living the dream

The dreamers of the day are dangerous, for they may act out their dreams with open eyes to make them possible.
Lawrence of Arabia

Going for the 900!

Has anybody heard of Tony Hawk?

Course you have. He's the most famous skateboarder in the world. And he's got a whole series of PlayStation games named after him. He's been going for years and he's still breaking records, innovating new tricks, showing all the whippersnappers the way it should be done!

I'm not going to pretend that I'm some kind of skater, although my mum does possess some very dubious old photos of me plus helmet and board from about 1979! I even help out at the local skate park once a week but if you ask any of the kids there, they'll tell you that I've cunningly avoided ever getting on a ramp. I'm a great spectator, though, and I saw something not too long ago that totally grabbed me in the heart and gave me a lump in my throat.

It was while I was away on my honeymoon that I saw this amazing trick pulled by Tony Hawk. I was slobbing out in the big four poster bed, watching cable TV. It was the back end of the summer and every day we were getting the 'X Games' live – awesome stuff. Not just skateboarding but BMX-ing, Xtreme Moto Cross, Sky Surfing – the works! They were also showing clips of previous X Games tournaments, the really hot year being 1999 in San Francisco. They have a skateboard competition called 'Best Trick'. The man Tony was there, competing against all the top pros. He had nothing to prove, really; he already has the reputation for being number one but he wasn't resting on his laurels. It was a very special night. He decided that in this major contest, in front of a massive audience, he was going for 'the 900' – a 900-degree spin thrown on one of those huge halfpipe ramps.

The trick had never been done before in a professional tournament. In fact, the commentators thought that he was having a laugh when he went for it and ended up chewing the plywood three or four times. Then they realised he was serious. He tried again, then again. Slowly, people noticed that something special was happening.

The camera went in close and you could see that his face was totally set. There was something in his eyes. There were about eight or nine other pro skaters competing and one by one, they got off their boards and cleared the stage. The other events drew to a close. The sky started getting dark. The floodlights flickered and hummed into life. Very soon, the whole stadium was watching Tony

Hawk attempt the trick that the experts had said was impossible. Two and a half full spins high in the air, defying gravity and centrifugal force. Flying blind and, in many ways, having true faith. Landing this trick would be the skating equivalent of landing on the moon.

I started to get a knot in my belly as he went for attempts eight, nine and ten. The sheer physical strain was beginning to show in the veins on his neck and the sweat on his face. The other skaters were lined up along the top of the ramps, kneeling behind their boards. I even saw one guy put his hand on Tony's head, as if praying for him! The tension was so massive, it was becoming painful. I eventually started to think that it was going to be the biggest embarrassment in history.

Attempt number eleven. He completes the spin, connects the wheels with the wood, then wipes out in a backwards skid. Pretty soon, the event marshals are going to have to call time.

Attempt twelve. The sky is totally black. The crowds are totally silent. Hawk is totally focussed. He drops in like a diving bird, the thrust drives him high up the other side of the pipe, back down again picking up every last bit of the necessary speed, up, down, UP... 180, 360, 540, 720, 900... feet still gripping the board... trucks and wheels buckle with the strain as he lands it, he holds it, yes, HE HOLDS IT! YES! EVERYBODY GOES WILD!!! PILE ON!!! PARTY!!! And I jump up out of bed and run around the room punching the air, to my wife's bewilderment.

I never thought I could get so fired up watching a bloke scoot around on a bit of wood but it really was awesome. Reflecting on this spine-tingling moment, I've recognised three really crucial things which I want to underline for you – things for you to learn as a young evangelist, whatever dream you're reaching for in life.

It Always Starts with a Dream

Following the feature, there was an interview in which Tony said that the first time he'd attempted the trick was ten years previously. He'd talked with his mates about it and they'd laughed at him. But he saw it inside him. He saw himself gliding through the air. He knew one day he'd do it.

I believe that there is a unique and individual dream for everyone reading this book. Maybe you have it all very clearly defined – when, where and how. For some of you, it's fuzzy. Just a feeling inside. A sense of destiny. Or perhaps you dream about all kinds of things and find your future really difficult to pin down.

As I read my Bible, I see all those types of people. Take, for instance, Hannah; you can find her story at the beginning of 1 Samuel. Hannah knew – and she knew that she knew – that all she wanted in life was a son. It was a medical impossibility, a matter for God alone. Or there was shifty young Jacob, gripped by a promise bigger than himself, but frustrated, as it always seemed just beyond his reach. And, of course, there was impulsive disciple Peter, chasing a different dream every day, spending a lot of energy but not really getting very far. In the natural they were all destined for nothing but disappointment, but they were all taken hold of by God to lead overcoming lives that would shout of his greatness and grace. I'm confident that God has a dream and a destiny for you all. God doesn't short-change anybody. We've all got our own '900' to reach for!!!

The Secret Place

I found out that Tony Hawk had actually pulled off the 900 degree trick five times in private practice sessions. Just him and his board. You can translate that straight into Christian experience because God just loves that quality in people. He's on the lookout for it all the time. People who will put in the hours in the secret place, not just in front of the crowds.

I don't consider myself a great example but I know that I would be nowhere today if I hadn't practised this principle. If I hadn't spent time walking the streets of Manchester, praying and listening to God. If I hadn't snuck out late at night to drive around Manchester and proclaim God's reign over the high places. I didn't find compassion for people in a daydream, I had to spend time with down-and-outs and let myself be vulnerable. The only right I have to direct my voice to young people has been earned through hours spent with bored and lonely teenagers on the estates of this city. What I'm trying to tell you is that when I say it happens in the secret place – that doesn't just mean your bedroom. Get out there!

Jesus spent thirty years in complete obscurity. Then he spent a chunk of his ministry trekking round rural Galilean and Judaean villages nobody was really bothered about, before finally making himself known in the mega-city, Jerusalem. Do yourself a favour and learn to be invisible. Learn to pray, 'God, I'm going to serve you with all my heart, all my life, and if nobody hears about it, so much the better!'

In Isaiah 49:2, there is a declaration which sums up this experience,

'...he made me into a polished arrow and concealed me in his quiver...'

The picture is of God, the great warrior, long-bow in hand and arrows strapped to his back. Each one of those arrows is a person he has chosen for himself, someone he has been working on over time, straightening, strengthening and polishing. Each arrow is waiting in the quiver for selection with high anticipation, praying for the moment when the master's hand will touch it and draw it into the daylight, ready to send a fatal shot to the heart of the enemy. Of course, many times his hand takes instead one of those around us, or he takes us out only to do a bit more straightening or polishing. It's true to say, though, better to be found ready in the secret place than to waste your time anywhere else.

No Overnight Success

Lastly, for Tony and for each one of us, it won't all happen straight away – which doesn't mean that it won't be sudden. The pattern of the Bible is not one of overnight successes. Look at Joshua, David and Daniel. Their learning curve started young, stayed steep, and didn't ever go flat. In my case, I must be honest, I've dreamed of talking on big stages like *Planet Life* for 20 years and it's just started to happen. In the process of getting there, I've made some right cock-ups. Every aspiring preacher's nightmare has become a reality. I've spoonerised, I've offended people, I've waffled, I've frozen up, my mind's gone blank, I've burst into tears, I think I've probably even been openly heretical and in danger of being struck by lightning... but I have a dream and it's coming real. I've seen my '900' and I'm going for it. I'll continue to graft away in the secret place but increasingly, it's going public. My dream is that, as I speak, God will form a window in each individual listening soul that permits a good long gaze into heaven and that faith will ignite, as God in all his power and all his love becomes more real than my own breath.

Ask yourself right now, is it time to take a risk? I've never seen a dream become real without a little bit of risk. When you take a risk, you find out what's for real and what's just fake. Maybe now is the right time for you to bring your dream into the open and to accelerate to the next level.

When we launched *Xcelerate*, the training school for raw young evangelists, it was because we recognised that there's a new thing going on. The pace has shifted in the world and we have to respond. Young people are itching to live a life that counts. Don't just take my word for it; listen to these guys who were on our first ever course. While they were with us, they wrote down personal mission statements and now they're all over the country, taking bold steps towards living them out.

'To reach my full potential in God, so I am fully prepared, so God can use me to impact the world' – Michelle, 19, Manchester

'To keep close and become closer to God, learning how to stay strong and uncompromising; to learn how to build friends more confidently, and to become an infectious Christian' – Becky, 19, Leicestershire

'To draw closer to Jesus, grow a heart for the lost and share the glory of God' – Carl, 23, Cardiff

'To get more into God, a foundation in Christ, to have faith in action' – Simon, 19, Cambridgeshire

'Building a stronger relationship with God, being a witness to the community; it is the start of a new thing in my life, a stepping stone for what's coming next' – Jiska, 21, Holland

'To be obedient, even if it means pain. To walk on my own, though I stumble in the rain. To live by faith, for that is truly gain' – Robbie, 19, Gloucestershire

> If your dream is from God, he will make sure that you achieve it.

Xcelerate might be for you if you're in your late teens or early twenties. If you dream to reach the world, if you've been grafting away in the secret place where nobody is watching, then you might want to spend some time in Manchester with us. We've been there. I really do believe that I'm talking to that Tony Hawk Generation who have that dream inside and are determined to pull it off, no matter how many times they fall down on the way.

And, you know, this is more than just chasing dreams. The Bible is very clear on this. We will have victory. When we pull our personal '900', there is a crown waiting and it's worth more than any X-Games medal. If you don't believe me, take a look at 1 Corinthians 9:25:

'Everyone who competes in the (X) games (!) goes into strict training. They do it to get a crown that will not last; but we do it to get a crown that will last for ever.'
Cool.

Let's have a ten-second recap at this point...

Success starts with a dream. It's developed in the secret place. If you persevere, you will break through. You can do it. If your dream is from God, he will make sure that you achieve it. When he starts a job, he brings it to completion.

The New Self

Although we recognise the power of the dream, we can't spend our lives being unreal. In fact, our dreams in God will never be anything *but* dreams if we neglect the disciplines which enable us to lead Christian lives which are fulfilling to us and pleasing to God.

You might want to flick to Ephesians 4:17 at this point and get that highlighter pen busy.

'So I tell you this, and insist on it in the Lord, that you must no longer live as everyone else in the world, in the futility of their thinking. They are darkened in their understanding and separated from the life of God because of the ignorance that is in them due to the hardening of their hearts. Having lost all sensitivity, they have given themselves over to sensuality so as to indulge in every kind of impurity, with a continual lust for more.'

Three things stand out to me in this text. There's a problem, a result and a reason.

'No longer live in futile thinking.' Oooohhhh! 'There's no point...' That's a big problem for a lot of people, especially in the emerging generation. Over the last five years, I've watched a lot of my mates going absolutely nowhere and getting there pretty quickly. Some would say that this is a modern problem, a lazy attitude, giving up too easily. That's partly true, but the philosophical origins of this attitude go way back. Solomon was bugged to bits by it. His book Ecclesiastes is filled with disappointment and frustration.

'Everything is meaningless, a chasing after the wind.' You'll never be happy or

fulfilled with that sort of attitude. Far from it:

'Thinking like that separates you from God', it says in verse 18, and darkens your understanding. It clouds your judgement and affects your life on every level. You take things for granted and don't value the good things you have, such as families and friends and most of all, God.

Why do people end up like this? The text says it's because of ignorance, due to the hardening of hearts. That's one of the saddest things you can find in a person, when his heart has gone stony and cold, iced over like a pond in winter. Nothing can get in and nothing can get out. It's even more upsetting when the person in question is thirteen or fourteen years old.

Dress for the Dream

That's the bad news. If we turn back to our Bibles, we can find out the good news. *'You, however, did not come to know Christ that way. Surely you heard of him and were taught in him in accordance with the truth that is in Jesus. You were taught, with regard to your former way of life, to put off your old self, which is being corrupted by its deceitful desires; to be made new in the attitude of your minds; and to put on the new self, created to be like God in true righteousness and holiness.'* (Eph 4:20–24)

Manchester has stacks and stacks of skaters. I've not met any of them who can pull tricks like Tony Hawk's but nevertheless, they do take their sport seriously. Especially the clothes. These days, ninety per cent of the fashion on the street is influenced in some way, shape or form by skate culture. The dress code is of top priority. That's what this passage is saying to us. The first bit we read detailed the ins and outs of the problem with three major points. This part contains the solution to the problem, also in three handy stages.

Stage one, verse 22 – put off your old self

Stage two, verse 23 – be made new in the attitude of your minds

Stage three, verse 22 – put on the new self

Let's take a closer look at these.

Put Off Your Old Self

The Amplified Bible digs deeper into this verse. It says:

'Strip yourselves of your former nature – put off and discard your old unrenewed self – which characterised your previous manner of life and becomes corrupt through lusts and desires which spring from delusion.'

The Bible isn't talking here about your Timberland jumper or your Kookai trousers; it's on about what you look like on the inside. Just as you wear clothes on the outside, you also wear clothes on the inside. Most of you should know that, but do you take as much time over the right internal outfit as you do over the external one? Each one of us, even the Queen, has a private side to their nature which is totally offensive to God, with stinking thoughts and habits clinging to our personalities like a sweaty old shell suit. Things such as jealousy, anger, selfishness, greed, lying, bigheadedness, spite, guilt and bad language. You wouldn't walk around with clothes like that on the outside, so why do you put up with them on the inside, which is, after all, where it really matters?

I saw a photo a little while back, a graduation photo, on the 'Hall of Fame' at a Bible College. I looked again and thought, 'Hold on a minute.' There was a guy, with big hair, dark glasses, deep pink shirt with a white tie, big cheesy grin – yep, it was one my pastors! Thankfully, he's not still wearing the same clothes that he had on fifteen years ago; he'd not only stink to high heaven, he'd be well out of fashion and definitely still single. There would have to be something wrong if you left yourself to rot like that. Jesus is the one who gives us the ability to take off our old lives and chuck them in the skip; your old life isn't even good enough to be dry-cleaned and given to Oxfam. Bin it. You have to look at yourself in the mirror, in the cold light of day and say, 'Jesus, thanks for opening my eyes and showing me what a state I'm in. I'm gonna take off this selfishness, this guilt, this spitefulness…' Try looking at it this way. Christ has made it possible to discard that old jacket but he's not going to come and help you with the zip!

So where do you go from here? What if your whole life was built up around feeling guilty and being mardy and greedy? You need something new.

Be Made New in the Attitude of Your Minds

Taking the Amplified version again, it says:

'...be constantly renewed in the spirit of your mind – having a fresh mental and spiritual attitude.'

You find lots of cool ideas like this in the Bible. The problems start when you try and put them into practice. How exactly do you get your mind renewed? Do you get the Yellow Pages and look it up, K – L – M...

'Ah, yes, M. Magicians, Market researchers, Mechanics, Milkmen, ah, Mind renewers, see also Head Transplanters and Brain Exchange.'

It's not going to be so easy, is it? You're going to have to put a bit of effort in. If you read the rest of Ephesians 4 and 5, you'll find loads of practical things to do which will help refresh you, mentally and spiritually, I won't mention them all but I've picked some out which should be helpful – things you could start doing right now.

In Chapter 4, see verse 25: Speak truthfully. Verse 26: Don't let the sun go down while you're angry. Verse 27: Don't give the Devil a foothold. Verse 29: Speak to build up, not knock down. Verse 30: Don't grieve the Holy Spirit. Verse 32: Be kind and forgive. In Chapter 5, see verse 6: Don't be deceived by empty words. Verse 19: Sing and make music in your heart to the Lord. Verse 20: Always give thanks.

It's amazing how, when you get your head sorted out, the rest of your body follows. Romans 8:6 says:

'The mind of sinful people is death, the mind controlled by the Spirit is peace.'

It's the Holy Spirit who empowers you to do all this, helps you and guides you, puts you on the right track. That's why it says in the list in verse 30, 'don't grieve the Holy Spirit.' The Holy Spirit is always with you, so be considerate and don't ignore him. Would you ignore your best friend? Would you like it if he ignored you?

Put on the New Self

The full quotation is 'put on the new self, created to be like God in true righteousness and holiness.'

This is what we all need to replace our old flares and platforms that are smelly and worn through. The new self – what is it? We already touched on it in Chapter 4.

'...clothe yourselves with compassion, kindness, humility, gentleness and patience. Bear with each other and forgive whatever grievances you may have against one another. Forgive as the Lord forgave you. And over all these virtues put on love, which binds them all together in perfect unity.' (Col 3:12–14)

Compassion, kindness, humility, gentleness, patience, forgiveness and love.

Consider this list carefully. Imagine you're getting dressed. Nice clean pants of Compassion. Hook up the bra of Kindness (you lads can substitute socks there!) Big phat jeans by 'Humility Denim'. T-shirt with a nifty little 'Gentleness' logo and a pair of Patience shell-toes. 'Forgiveness' is the label on the jacket and we pick up the can of Love, giving the whole outfit a good spray! We may jest now but don't underestimate how serious these characteristics are; they're your new clothes, robes of righteousness, *'created to be like God in true righteousness and holiness'*.

PS

As a post-script to all this, comes a bit of inside information. It comes from painful experience and heavy embarrassment. *Don't put the old self back on!*

Do you ever get sentimental about a certain item in your wardrobe, a pair of jeans or a leather jacket, lucky pants. I'm going to give away my age here but I used to have one of those 'Tom Cruise' flying jackets, the brown leather one with the fur collar. It was about three sizes too big for me but I didn't care. I got it when I was fourteen and it never left my back for about five years. Other coats came and went, but this jacket was part of me – the reassuring smell, the comfy fit with the fraying cuffs, the crooked zip, the lining coming away under the sleeve. I loved it dearly. I think I've still got it somewhere.

The link is, when someone is born again, he receives new spiritual clothes, but there is always the attraction of that comfy old pride and that well-worn selfishness. I still find that part of me wants to go back to that old life, but I can't. It's not that simple. It's like putting one jacket on top of another. The new self which God delivers looks fantastic and nobody really wants to take it off. So the only choice is to try and wear both selves at the same time. You must know the feeling. A moment of temptation comes. You're out with your old mates and just for chapter six

a while, you begin to slip the old self back on. But you look like a right Rodney. You feel uncomfortable, self-conscious, a prat, not your old self at all, really. Everyone else can see it, too.

Don't put your old self back on again. Take it from me; it doesn't work. You feel uncomfortable and you look like a prat. God has a better self for you than that old one. Put on your new self and wear it proudly.

chapter
seven
gob on legs!

My one purpose in life is to help people
find a personal relationship with God,
which, I believe, comes through
knowing Christ. I will never do anything
as long as I live except preach the
gospel and intend to do that as long as
God gives me breath.
Billy Graham

Andy Asks, 'What Happened to Preaching?'

In this world of quick fixes and sound bites, preaching seems a stupid thing to do. Frequently I've stood up at the end of a noisy, chaotic *Tribe* gig and thought – 'What a fool I look, compared to all the flashing lights, booming bass and dance routines!' But time and again, I've witnessed God turn up and use my foolish preaching to point young people to Jesus and I've then seen those very young people become Christians and come alive to God. What an awesome privilege!

I'll never forget my first Billy Graham crusade at a packed Anfield Football Stadium, waiting in keen anticipation to hear the great man bring his message. After about ten minutes, I became convinced that I was about to witness the very first Billy Graham rally where no one was saved. His talk was not very dynamic and seemed little more than a string of scriptures tied together with a few analogies. But then it came to the time for his appeal and the evangelist's anointing kicked in – in the most dynamic way! Thousands flocked forward to receive Christ, including, to my amazement, the woman sitting next to me – my mother-in-law. What a bizarre thing preaching the gospel really is!

Don't get me wrong; it's not that I don't believe in being wildly creative and radical in our presentation of the gospel – I do, but I believe even more in preaching the simple gospel to the lost. In fact, I believe that when you bring the two together, you have a dynamic combination that our God loves to use. Matty boy has pulled together some research in this chapter which will help all you budding preachers make the most of every opportunity that comes your way.

> In this world of quick fixes and sound bites, preaching seems a stupid thing to do.

**chapter
seven**

Making God Visible

It can be quite baffling for a believer when family and friends don't recognise or acknowledge what is clearly God at work – blessing, answer to prayer, divine appointments and all that stuff. As disciples, we are those who know daily interaction with him in our lives. It 's normal, it's just life. While I was at Uni, I could chat with the weirdest members of the freak show which went under the banner of 'Fine Arts Department' about a transcendent God, infinite and removed from this created order but it always got tricky when I dropped in that 'I had a chat with him this morning.' They didn't believe that he could be with us, they didn't want to admit that he is with us and to be honest, I wouldn't blame God for wanting to stay away from us! So many times, I got all knotted up inside about it, imagining how different it would be if El-Shaddai would just show up with a puff of smoke and an Alan Partridge 'AHA!'

Philip Yancey gives some serious attention to this often problematic creator/creation relationship in his book *Reaching for the Invisible God*. He uses the illustration of a father playing hide and seek with his child. The ultimate enjoyment of the game, of course, is contained in the buzz of finding and being found. There's also a little throwaway line in there, which I've heard used quite a lot by all kinds of people, even during an interview with Simon Mayo! Credited to a medieval Christian mystic chap called Meister Eckhart, it reads like this, 'God is like a person who clears his throat while hiding and so gives himself away.' Nice idea – but what does that make the cross? One hell of a sneeze! The apostle Paul teaches, in Romans chapter 1, that God can be seen, *'For since the creation of the world, God's invisible qualities – his eternal power and divine nature – have been clearly seen, being understood from what has been made, so that men are without excuse.'*

That is so true. His divine nature is revealed all around us and should be evident in our lives, too. This is where testimony makes its impact. Stories of God in our lives can be dead useful when helping to focus people's eyes towards him. People need to trust that God exists and they need to know that Jesus came, but, more than that, we must help them see that by his Spirit, God is here. A good communicator – and I don't mean a slick talker; there's a difference – will lead the listener from this platform of understanding to the next level. Yes, God is *immanent*, all around us, but he is also *imminent*, available to us right now!

Last Christmas, hundreds of churches in Manchester laid down their umpteen different approaches to JC's big day and united around a single theme which tied into a high profile TV and billboard campaign, *Campaign for Real Christmas*. I caught a passion for this campaign because it's an *Urgency of Truth* thing, a realignment in the public domain of our wonderful festival which has been hijacked by the breweries and the credit card companies. It was one of those fantastic but, tragically, all too rare occasions when the church forgot about being 'local' and started being Zion, the city of God. Our building, a big old bread factory in the city centre, was packed out with tons of guests and I had the privilege of explaining why we celebrate God the Son entering human history, his coming to declare and demonstrate the true meaning of life. As an evangelist who loves to preach but doesn't get all that much chance, I milked every moment they gave me, doing all I could to paint a true picture of Jesus. The hope I held in my heart was that as the crowd caught a glimpse of him, they would be captivated forever by his beauty. Never the same. I hope that God gives you opportunities like that. I'm sure he will. When he does, this chapter might help you squeeze the juice out of them.

The Communicator's Toolkit

As long as people like getting together in groups and crowds, which is likely to be for a long time yet, then there'll be a place for preaching the gospel. Lots of young people turn up on *Xcelerate* thinking that they are designed for one-to-one evangelism and look utterly mortified when anyone suggest anything to the contrary. The simplest solution is to point them to Jeremiah 1:6 and let the Holy Spirit do the rest!

No one's suggesting that speaking in front of ten, or a hundred, or a thousand, or even ten thousand people won't scare the pants off you, but if six and a half billion people are going to hear about Jesus without crowds being reached then somebody's going to have to work very hard one-to-one! The rest of this chapter picks up that challenge with a collection of communication tips for the budding preacher. They aren't all super-spiritual; in fact, most are handy hints pinched from sales and marketing training manuals and stuff like that.

The Gap

The basic theory which we're going to explore here is known as 'The Communication Gap'. The gist of it is that we aren't telepathic. No shock there, okay; well, even those of us who think that we're excellent communicators are actually very limited in all sorts of ways. Let's break it down. The simplest form of communication between people will involve one person being the sender and the other being the receiver. You and I could be sitting on the sofa; I'd be wearing a hat with a shiny badge on it saying 'Sender'; you'd sit there with your shiny badge saying 'Receiver'. OK. Got the image? Now I have to communicate to you. I rub my head and start to hum. I'm imagining a pink polar bear dancing round a zebra skin handbag. You are none the wiser. It's not good enough for me just to imagine it; I have to convey the message. I could do a mime, I could send you a text, or I could just say what I see. As well as a sender and a receiver, there must be a message. All right, that's still quite straightforward. Where it starts getting a bit tricky is when the communication becomes complex. Now we get into the area in which an effective evangelist needs to excel. What if the message I want to send is, 'I have a great sense of humour'? Should I just lean over and say, 'By the way, I'm extremely funny, you know'? You'll just think, 'No, you're not, you're an arrogant git.'

The key to communication, as any advertiser will tell you, is in the encoding and decoding of the message, the 'hidden persuaders'. Take your mobile phone, for instance. You tap in your text message and the words are digitally encoded by SMS, then fired to a mast somewhere, bounced off a satellite and through another transmitter before finally being decoded by your friend's mobile in the next classroom. Sender, message, encoded, decoded and received. Interpersonal communication is just the same. If I tell you a really good joke and make you laugh, then you're much more likely to receive my intended message properly, 'This is a funny guy, really good sense of humour.'

As we grow up, our ability to communicate complex feelings and emotions develops. We express ourselves in new ways, we develop relationships with deeper levels of intimacy and we are able to convey the 'real us', being more fully understood. Have you ever used the phrase, 'She got the wrong end of the stick'? It's a way of saying, 'My communication wasn't correctly decoded.' Many people have never got to grips with anything higher than childish means of interacting and so end up in constant arguments. For the record, I think that argument is the lowest form of communication. You can quote me on that if you like.

Of course, communication is not just about what you say. Scientific research shows that this is only a small part, dominated by much greater factors. Take a look at these 'Communication Statistics', taken from *the Sunday Times* 'Creating Success' series.

Verbal content, the words you use when you speak– 7%.
Vocal interest, the pace, tone and inflection of your voice – 38%.
Body language, what your persona is passively or actively suggesting – 55%.

It's amazing and quite scary at the same time, isn't it? Just consider how much more effective we could be as witnesses for God if we would take the time to send and receive human signals at these deeper levels. But just think of the extent to which the most amazing words in the world, even 'God-breathed' words straight from the Bible, can be undermined if we are mumbling, fidgeting and all that.

When I'm trying to relax I usually immerse myself in a computer game. I love those *SIM* games, *SIMCity* and the latest one – The *SIMS*. It's fantastic. You get to create people and control every part of their lives. Make breakfast, watch TV, water the plants, go to the loo – even strike up a romance! Don't get worried, I'm not a megalomaniac. I'm quite sane and I've got a certificate from my doctor to prove it. Anyway, to help your chosen characters get on in life, you can train them in all sorts of skills. If you want them to improve their 'charisma' rating, then you get them to talk to themselves in the mirror. Just one click and off they go – jabbering away until you tell them to stop. Here comes confession time, though; have you ever done it yourself? There you are in the bathroom, brushing your teeth. You put down your toothbrush and look intently at yourself in the mirror.

'Hi!' 'Hello.' 'Well, helllllllo.' 'Well, hellooooooooo.'

And you're off into fantasy chat-up line land! That's what we're talking about with vocal interest. A whopping 38% of communication. We do a session with our *Xcelerators* where we partner them up and get them to read great long bits of the Bible to each other and try to keep each other's interest vocally by playing with pace, volume and pitch, using different accents. If we're feeling really mean, we'll give them Leviticus as a text – let's face it, nobody can listen to that for very long under normal circumstances without falling asleep. You should try it. While you're at it, consider this; research also shows that people will often perceive someone with a slower paced, lower toned voice as being powerful and credible while those with faster, more high-pitched voices will come across as enthusiastic, yes, but also lightweight and potentially untrustworthy.

Many people understand the concept of body language but few people actively pay attention to it. Even fewer actively use body language as a tool in communication. Now, clearly, we're not all going suddenly to enlist on *Creative Mime Evangelism* courses. The main point to catch about body language is to learn to let it flow with, rather than against, the content of what you are saying. The hectic flappy arm brigade do risk unravelling their own words and coming across as being a few geese short of a gaggle.

Have you ever seen video footage of Billy Graham doing an appeal? As he reaches his big conclusion, he will lean forward and make a powerful double finger point into the sky. It's an unmissable gesture and demands attention to what he has just said. There'll be a dramatic pause, then repetition. Content and expression in dynamic co-operation. He allows his whole person to be used by God as a means of conveying the message. What's even more amazing is that his communication is just as spot on one-to-one as it is to a hundred thousand people.

Before we move on, I want to touch on one more thing. First impressions last. Any stand-up comedian will tell you about the 'The Magic Minute': in the first five to ten seconds, everyone watching has formed a subconscious opinion. Over the next fifty to fifty-five seconds, those opinions are confirmed and qualified but rarely undone. Whatever situation you meet someone in, you'll be subject to those same judgements. The first minute really counts; it can set you up for hours and hours of quality time. A smile, some non-threatening eye contact (don't be eyeing up anywhere else, for goodness' sake!), respecting personal space while remaining confident and alert. It all goes to getting well received in that first minute. Trust me, I'm an evangelist.

Techniques and Tools

Here's some ideas you might choose to take on board if you find yourself in the situation where you have to prepare for an up-front talk, maybe to your disenchanted youth group or to a school assembly of bouncing hyperactive Year Sevens.

Visualisation: Sit down and imagine that you are there doing it – loving it – being effective! If you can get a look at the room first, then get in there while it's empty and have a pace around. Think carefully about the response you expect as you draw out the different aspects of your talk.

Framework: Know how your talk fits together. What are the different elements, how do they link together? Where will you slot in creative communication devices and how?

Mapping: If you are preparing a longish talk, anything over about fifteen minutes, you should probably let people know where it's going. It helps them to tune in and gauge how much more they've got to listen to! For instance, you might be talking about 'The meaning of being male'. You would map it out right at the start of your introduction like this:

'Over the next twenty minutes, we'll be looking at what it means to be male. We'll begin by looking at excess body hair then we'll move on to nasty smells, spend a little while considering the challenge of fixing shelves with Sellotape before finally concluding with the dissection of a live specimen.'

Visuals: Even the simplest of visuals will enhance any presentation massively, not only engaging the audience but also providing you with convenient milestones at which to take a breather and have a quick glance at your notes.

'Have a look at this picture and think for a minute about just how many pies went into the construction of that serious trouser overhang.'

Activations: There are also some astounding statistics which detail the impact of setting activities as memory aids during presentations. You've done this sort of thing loads of times:

'Get yourself into twos and threes and all stand on your heads singing "Auld Lang Syne."'

It works, as long as the activation bears some kind of relevance to the subject being dealt with.

Questions: Inviting questions can be really helpful, especially when there is any room for confusion or misunderstanding or if what you're saying is new or hard to get to grips with. The golden rules are, 'Listen, repeat and close.'

Listen, or you'll end up looking like a right wally, as I did the other day when I was interviewing Andy on stage at the big launch of a new EDEN project. I asked him a question in front of the crowd and expected him to go off into a Hawthorne rant for at least five minutes. Instead, he wrapped it up quickly and fired another question back to me. I'd drifted off and begun lining up the next point. Of course, I was caught right off my guard and much laughter ensued at my expense.

Repeat, for the benefit of others in the room and to make sure that you've heard the question correctly so that you can give an appropriate answer.

Close. Wherever possible, try to deal with the question fully, especially if you feel that it is genuine and will benefit the whole audience. Leaving issues open-ended can mean that people will go away with unresolved issues which will work against the value of all the good things you've said.

Attention Grabbers

The human mind is full of so much junk at any one moment that connecting with its attention is a struggle all of its own. We can learn a lot from advertisers here; they know this all too well. To be able to affect our behaviour, advertisements must first enter our minds. We do not notice and cannot remember everything we see. It would be absurd to suggest that anyone could. When we are scanning a crowd for a familiar face, we actually discern only a small percentage of what appears in our field of vision. Our unconscious observation systems prevent us being overwhelmed by irrelevant information. The proper psychological term for it is 'Selective Perception'. Advertising guru Winston Fletcher describes it more completely as, *'The extraordinary mechanism by which our eyes, in concert with our brains, pick out and notice particular items from the morass of visual data which assails them at every waking moment.'* As we all know, the marketers will try absolutely anything to get our attention. I'm not suggesting that you paint yourself orange and learn to juggle but here's a small selection of tips and tricks to help break you through.

The Outrageous: Whenever you get up to talk, you can always check that your audience is awake by making a brash statement which will hopefully be true and have some tenuous link to your talk.

'I wrote fifty per cent of this book while drifting on a life raft in the North Sea."

Negatives: Any issue can be looked at from a whole range of perspectives. There's always a good side and a bad side. It's not necessarily always the good news which gets the headlines. Careful, though; it can be counter-productive to get into gratuitous shock tactics.

Quotations: They may never have heard of you but a quote from a well-respected or well-recognised person can do a great job of setting the tone and creating useful associations.

Jokes: Brilliant, as long as they're funny! Have you heard the one about...

Topical References: Depending on the audience and the strength of your reference, you can have people hanging off your words. For twenty-four hours before an important talk, you should have one eye on the news headlines. If there's a story around that links with what you're about to say then slot it in. Remember, though, that nobody want to hear yesterday's news, as I discovered to my horror when opening a youth preach with 'WAAAASSUP!'

It was a totally cringy tumbleweed moment. At an event two weeks earlier, the same opening had worked a treat. The world moves fast!

Teasers: You don't have to give away all your best material in the first two minutes. Good communicators not only grab attention, they hold it. You may choose to reveal your material a bit at a time, creating some tension and mystery about where you're going next. Don't drag it out too long, though, or they might just get bored and start secretly playing 'Snake' on their mobiles. I've never done that while someone's been preaching, honest, Your Honour, a bloke down the pub told me he saw someone doing it...

Penny Droppers

In the course of your talk, you'll no doubt have a series of points to make. If you're adopting the neo-classic style, there'll be three of them and they'll all begin with

the letter P! Not many people with a sanity rating of 'fair' or above stand in front of people and gas on for the sake of it. *Your point* is the point. If they don't get the point, then what was the point? Several oral devices can be employed to ensure that the all-important point is received intact.

Stories: Repetition is the communicator's friend and ally, but being repetitive is certainly not. Stories can be a great way of making the same point in different ways. Watch the clock, though, as when you get going on a good story, time can just disappear. Also, if your subject is personal and first-hand, so much the better, I stay away from stories that have 'done the circuit'. Keep 'em fresh and keep 'em snappy.

Examples: We're in real Jesus-land here; the examples he used were so clever. The pearl of great price, the buried treasure, fish, sheep, weddings. Always consider who you're talking with. JC didn't talk about fish in Jerusalem, or sheep in Galilee. Likewise, you probably won't use the example of David Beckham's glorious free kick to the British Legion Widows' coffee morning.

Statistics: Some people are far more cerebral than emotional. If you want to get through to a bunch of boffins, you might try more qualified research than puppy-dog tales. If you are going to use stats, always try to quote the source. Unqualified figures aren't really worth wasting your breath on.

Concept Tools

Easy to remember. Before your talk, gargle with TCP. Well, that's not strictly true, a nice greasy bag of crisps will actually do your vocal chords the world of good. Smokey bacon are best, I find. No, TCP stands for tweaking, chunking and perspective.

Tweaking is the continuous fine-tuning of your content right up to and even during your preach. If you're anything like me or Andy, you'll be scribbling stuff out and writing new stuff in even as you're being welcomed on to the stage.

Chunking is the knack of breaking the talk into bite-sized chunks that are easier to swallow one at a time than in a great lump. You can 'chunk up' or 'chunk down'! Either start with a big point then break it down into smaller subheadings, or begin with a series of mini-points and build them into a huge revelation.

Perspective, so often overlooked, is the main reason why evangelists need to be part of a team rather than loose cannons. Examine what you are going to say from multiple points of view. Ask people their opinions about anything that could be dodgy or misheard. Just because it makes sense to you doesn't mean that anyone else is going to have a clue what you're on about!

Prepare Yourself!

Over and above all these tips and techniques, remember that this is not a science, it is a passion. We don't do it in our own strength, we do it in God's strength. I do believe that we should invest our talents just as the word teaches us, but it shouldn't become an obsession. My old boss, Andrew Belfield, swears that the great preachers spend more time preparing themselves than their material. You can slave forever over notes and research but unless you are dwelling in the secret place of the most high, you risk losing the lot. God is with you. Go for it.

chapter
seven

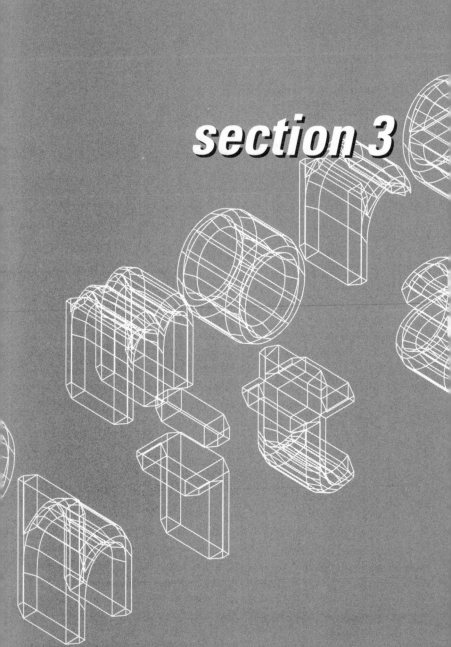

section 3

no more
hit and run

In this section, we'll glide over the twenty-first century landscape and map out the opportunities and dangers which lie ahead on the evangelist's journey. We'll weigh the baggage, find a seat in the departure lounge and anticipate the future. 'No more hit and run' is the slogan screaming silently from our T-shirts. Summed up in those few short words is a genuine concern over the shortcomings of common evangelistic strategy and a cool-headed commitment to do whatever it takes to win this generation in the days ahead.

Have you ever found yourself sitting, listening to someone who you've respected for ages, but sensing a creeping guilty feeling because you just aren't excited about hearing the same old ideas again, dressed up in a slightly different costume? Something inside is saying, 'But that's not what it's like in the world I'm living in!'

You're not alone; I've been there, and so have tons of other young people who all love God and want to live all out for him. Sadly, those feelings can be really tricky to articulate. The right moment never comes or it spills out in the wrong way. Cracks start appearing in once-sound relationships. It really shouldn't have to be that way. Try to learn early that change will interrupt your life every day – learn to flow with it.

Jesus taught his disciples to embrace change. In the Upper Room, he prepared them for the most abrupt and shocking change they would ever face – his own brutal execution. They were going to have to change to live life without his earthly company. Luke records the words of Jesus as he pulls a huge policy U-turn on them.

'Then Jesus asked them, "When I sent you without purse, bag or sandals, did you lack anything?"

"Nothing," they answered.

He said to them, "But now if you have a purse, take it, and also a bag; and if you don't have a sword, sell your cloak and buy one." ' (Luke 22:35,36)

The *Message Bible* paraphrases the dialogue really well.

'Then Jesus said, "When I sent you out and told you to travel light, to take only the bare necessities, did you get along all right?"

"Certainly," they said, "We got along just fine."

He said, "This is different. Get ready for trouble. Look to what you'll need; there are difficult times ahead. Pawn your coat and get a sword." '

Not too long ago, a young evangelist could probably get dressed in culturally relevant clothes, turn up at a culturally relevant event, preach a culturally relevant message, pray some culturally relevant prayers, jump back in a culturally relevant car and drive away singing culturally relevant songs of praise. Drive where? Into culturally relevant nowhere. This is different. Relevance has been overtaken by presence. You need to be there.

About a year ago, a couple of our mates came down to *Xcelerate* from Hull. Jarrod and Paul are fantastic young guys, overflowing with God. You can see it in their eyes. Between them, they've got a sack of stories which really deserve to be printed one of these days. Paul, in particular, shared something with us that I think would slot in here really well. I called him just the other day to double-check the details and he's cool with me passing it on to you.

There was this middle-aged woman, trying to tread water in life's choppy seas. She'd known God years back, but allowed herself to get dragged into a whole lot of stuff that had done her no good. She'd really lost her way. When she got through to Paul, by ringing his church and asking for help, she opened up to him about where she was really at. She'd shacked up some time ago with a local character in the scrap metal business. Things were far from perfect. A friend of theirs, a younger guy, had started using smack. In no time, he'd got hooked and things had become desperate. All she could think to do was ring the church. Paul agreed to pay them a visit.

Their lounge wasn't likely to get featured in Wallpaper magazine but sitting in armchair number one, with addict friend spaced out in armchair number two and the woman and her fella propped up on the sofa, Paul knew he was in the right place. During the next hour, God made himself known in amazing ways. Paul was able to describe, by word of knowledge (as in spiritual gift), all the twists and fractures in the young man's life and relationships. He had a chance to pray for them, right there and then, really simply and naturally... well, supernaturally. You see, the Holy Spirit decided to take them all out cold. Paul could only sit and watch in amazement as God performed his invisible work.

Pretty stunning, isn't it? And there's more – and here's what really makes the difference. Paul didn't just say a polite 'Cheerio' and rush back to the office to update the salvation counter on his ministry website. He promised to return. He made sure that the breakthrough process which started that day had the opportunity to continue. At that moment, he didn't know everything that would be involved. He didn't know that it would mean arriving at the guy's bedsit with cleaning products to make order out of the squalor. He didn't know that it would mean disposing of the needles and feeding the guy some proper meals. He didn't know that it would mean taking hours on end opening up the Bible and answering difficult questions. He just knew that he needed to be there to be Jesus.

'No more hit and run' is just that. It's the pulse taken from Isaiah 58:

'Spend yourself on behalf of the poor... satisfy the needs of the oppressed.'

Maybe you should have a look at that before you flick the page to the next chapter.

the tribes

Wake up faith, wake up passion, people dead over fashion
Fiddling while Rome burns and nations all around are crashing
Open sores and open wars and on report a righteous cause
The answer lies in our hands as we sit behind closed doors

Justin Thomas

The Adventure

My grandad, Albert, has always been a bit of a hero to me. He was a despatch rider in North Africa during the Second World War. As a kid, I would sit transfixed as he fed my fertile imagination with stories of taking top secret messages behind the German lines on his specially modified BSA. It probably explains my rather fanatical interest in all things James Bond, and why I see being a Christian as an adventure. But it's not just that. More than all the old war stories I've heard, more than all the Bond films I've watched – and believe me, I've seen them all at least a dozen times – I've read the Gospels! Talk about action – have you ever read Mark's Gospel? If they ever tried to do it justice on the silver screen, I think John Woo would have to direct it and it would star Mel Gibson or Bruce Willis as JC. The Gospels rock! And so I have developed the belief that evangelists, in fact, not just evangelists but all disciples, should positively go looking for situations that are challenging and maybe even a bit hairy and scary. That's the way I like it. I like to be reminded that I need God.

A story that has inspired many of my crazier choices for God is found wrapped up in the short lives of Jim Elliot and his four mates Pete, Nate, Ed and Roger. You'll never read a more gripping account of personal courage and sacrifice in the quest to reach the unreached. Jim's widow, Elizabeth, draws together the journals and prayer diaries of these young men as they trek through the Amazon discovering new levels of trust in God as they go. Check this out. It's nearly fifty years old but the heartbeat is an eternal rhythm.

The woman was lying on a bamboo board, partly shielded from public view by two loosely hung blankets, and was attended by the 'midwife'. Gradually all became dark, the smouldering fires died to embers, and the families went to their boards for the night... They gave Tidmarsh and me a bed and we lay down as there was no sign of the baby's arrival; labour pains were still seven minutes apart. As the bamboo had none of the usually associated attributes of flexibility which it has in the minds of many, and as our shoes and pants were still wet from walking in the river, we were soon chilled... In the company of two mangy skeleton-ribbed dogs, we sat listening to the whine of crickets, the strange goose-like honking of the tree toads, the occasional waking of a child, the creaking of the bamboo as someone rolled over, and the periodic moans of the woman which rose shrilly to a short scream.

Gradually, as the pains increased and intensified, the girl rose to her knees and reached for the vine rope which hung from the ceiling above, intertwining her hands in the rope and lifting her body up when the pains came. For me, those small brown hands held high over the head, and the arms, lined with taut tendons, communicated something of the simplicity and yet binding custom of their means of giving birth. After she had passed the water, the pains waned and finally, the baby began to descend. The midwife gave a word, everybody woke up and moved sleepily to the corner and stood peering over the curtains. Privacy is a word and concept unknown...

Venancio, our cook, then stepped inside, grasped the girl by the shoulders and began shaking her violently, which he continued to do until the baby arrived, dropping half onto the banana leaves, half onto the earthen floor, a tiny frail thing attached to an intestine-like cord, motionless in the flickering kerosene light. It burped a couple of times, sputtered and cried, then adopted normal breathing. Tidmarsh stepped in to tie off the cord, and the midwife cut it with the sharp end of a bamboo stick...

Meanwhile, the mother continued in her martyr-like position, wincing and writhing under the continuing contractions. Tidmarsh committed the baby to the Lord in prayer.'

Heavy scenes! Pete Fleming and Dr Tidmarsh find themselves sharing a hut in the Amazon with a woman who is giving birth. How do we begin establishing a frame of reference for where they were? Probably by rewinding a few years and looking at the heartbeat that led them there. In the previous chapter of the book there is a scene, with Pete and his mate Jim, sailing into their destination port in Ecuador singing together:

'Faith of our Fathers, Holy Faith, We will be true to thee till death.'

They meant every word of it and proved it. Can you put yourself there? The cold the smoke, the screams, the foreign language, the bewildering customs. There they were, two young men, walking the razor blade of faith, by the grace of God managing to maintain balance. They were learning reality. Blood and guts reality, not shampoo and set Christianity. I love the bit 'Tidmarsh committed the baby to the Lord in prayer...'

They were out of their depth. They were *un-learning* all their pat answers, all their theological knowledge and all their western education. They were learning from scratch to be the message and in God's plan, they would need to go through such extreme experiences, because they were being prepared for greater things. In Pete's case, to die demonstrating the gospel to savage Indians. Pete stands now, in the great cloud of witnesses, cheering us on. Respect.

But what about those of us who have never felt a calling to noisy, smoky huts in the Amazon? Where will we find our adventure? Hold that thought.

Tribal World

Xcelerate has benefited hugely from the generosity of heart expressed by the *Pioneer DNA team*. Way back when our programme was just a twinkle in Andy Hawthorne's eye, they were willing to make time to give us the benefit of their experience in discipling young evangelists. The DNA team leader, Pete Gilbert has given us frequent input, explaining how the world we see around us relates to the world that we read about in the pages of the Bible. Here he gives some insight on this missionary theme of reaching lost tribes.

'There were staying in Jerusalem God-fearing Jews from every nation under heaven.' (Acts 2:5)

chapter eight

That's a great little phrase that comes again and again in Scripture. *"te ethne"* is the Greek phrase there – every nation. What does that word remind you of – *ethne*? That's right – ethnic. It's the root of our word ethnic, or ethnicity. And it doesn't just mean every nation – more exciting than that, it means – every 'people-group'. So for those of you who are called to go to other nations that's wonderful. But what about those of you who are called to stay here? Well, there's a common link in each case; you have to be called to go and you have to be called to stay. It's not a default thing. For those of you who are called to go, great, go to the other nations, and for those of you who are called to stay, great, because you're called to every people-group.

Te Ethne, to every people-group. That's actually the same phrase which you find in Matthew 28:16–20, the great commission; *'Go and make disciples – te ethne', of all the nations, but not just of all the nations… of all the people-groups as well.*

It's the same phrase that's used in Matthew 24:14, where Jesus says, *'But first, this glorious Gospel of the Kingdom must be preached – te ethne' –* to all the nations. And then again, the same phrase crops up wonderfully in Revelation 7:9, as a little demonstration that it will happen, it will work. In Revelation 7:9 John, speaking prophetically, says:

'and I saw before the throne of God representatives from every tribe and nation'.

So it actually works! Think about that when you're engaging in evangelism. Think about that when it's tough with the people-group that you're working with, because somebody's gonna get saved from that people-group. John has seen it, even if you haven't! The gospel does work; you sow so you will reap. Talk about motivation, this is kicking stuff!

Now, let's move on to verse 6:

'When they heard this sound, (the disciples speaking in tongues) a crowd came together in bewilderment, because each one heard them speaking in his own language.' (Acts 2:6)

The point I want to make about this verse is about the gifts of the Spirit; they are there for growth. If you were to analyse the diary of Christ, the Son of God, in his three years of public ministry, you'd find that eighty per cent of it was spent in evangelism, fifty per cent of that with individuals. This is the Son of God, connected, in friendship evangelism. He's called in Luke chapter 7, 'Friend of sinners'. The Greek word means 'one who personally embraces to himself'. If you analyse the Gospels, you would find that twenty-five per cent of them are devoted to signs and wonders, to the miraculous, to spiritual gifts, and their use is in the context of evangelism, not church meetings! If you add the book of Acts to that little analysis, the figure shoots up to thirty-three per cent.

Let me ask you a question here. When do you think, historically, that the church started? It's not a trick question… it was right here, at Pentecost. Where did it start, specifically? In Jerusalem and in the street! You see, for a lot of the time, many Christians have thought that the church started in the Upper Room. Depending on where and when you think the church was born will determine what you think it needs to carry on. If you think that the church was born in a room with four walls, then you'll tend to think that the church needs a room with four walls. Actually, the birth of the church didn't take place in the Upper Room but in the outdoor market. It took place outside four walls. It took place with a manifestation and a demonstration of the Spirit's power in gifts and signs and wonders. Its immediate effect was to win people from every tribe and tongue to Christ, the effect it still has today.

You may not be called to reach nations at the other end of the earth, so take a look around you. There are probably unreached tribes and people-groups which God wants you to reach at the other end of your high street.

Magnet in your Heart

I've not sailed the coast of South America like Pete Fleming and Dr Tidmarsh, but I do believe that there have been precious moments of devotion when there's been just me and God when I have made the same journey in my human heart, where I've sung that song of sacrificial commitment. Have you ever listened to a band called *Iona* – sort of dreamy, Celtic, folky stuff? It was actually one of their songs which brought me to that place.

'Shrouded in the sweetest grass I've ever known, this my earthly bed, my beloved home, but the voice that calls me to the far away, I can only trust, every word you say… and here I am, out on the edge of the world, with you.'

I vividly remember kneeling by my bed, just graduated from Uni. I'd done really well, better than I could have imagined. I was praying and worshipping and considering the future. It was one of those *'You can have anything you ask for, God – I'm not holding anything as my own, I'll go anywhere, do anything, just give me the word'* moments. I buried my head in the quilt and cried for about half an hour.

As it turned out, God didn't call me to the Amazon; he called me about two miles up the road to Wythenshawe, which was a bit disappointing, to be honest, but the point of no return had been reached. The ties had been cut, my life was in God's hands and I was about to learn that the Amazon jungle wasn't the only place that you find lost tribes! There's one more little quote that I'd like to nick from our jungle pioneer friends, a quote about first impressions – and remember, first impressions last.

'Indians immediately gathered all around me and I remembered a couple of faces from Tidmarsh's pictures, and felt a kind of pride in remembering. My first thought was, Yes, I can love these people.'

Love was where Pete's journey started. Not sloppy, earthly love but the gritty, magnetic *Agape* love. Love has a gravitational pull more powerful than the moon to the seas or the sun to the earth. Love drew Christ to *planet earth*. Love drew Pete to the Amazon. I like to think that love drew me to Wythenshawe. Where will it draw you? No matter how near or far it is, the attitude remains the same. God's love will be the magnet in your heart.

From Encounters to Relationships

Have you ever met a girl or a guy and thought 'Whooa!'

Before you know it you're chatting away, having a laugh and fluttering your eyelashes at each other. Actually, that's probably more fantasy than reality because those moments are typically awkward and embarrassing. In the days that follow, though, there is no doubt, your mind races and you're thinking about The Encounter.

What happens next? You don't just leave it, do you? Hopefully you got their mobile number and you can send them a flirty text...

GR8 MTG U 2 NITE SLEEP TITE C U xxx

Then you go to bed but in the morning, you've lost your memory. And I'm not talking about anything you might have been guzzling the night before. Just imagine how awful it would be if life were just a series of chance encounters and you never ever got to know anyone. Encounters in themselves can be fun, but compared to the richness of a relationship, they're a bit hollow.

Lots of people in the Gospels had encounters with Jesus; one such person was Nathanael, in John 1.

'Philip found Nathanael and told him, "We have found the one Moses wrote about in the Law, and about whom the prophets also wrote — Jesus of Nazareth, the son of Joseph."

"Nazareth! Can anything good come from there?" Nathanael asked. "Come and see," said Philip.

When Jesus saw Nathanael approaching, he said of him, "Here is a true Israelite, in whom there is nothing false."

"How do you know me?" Nathanael asked. Jesus answered "I saw you while you were still under the fig-tree before Philip called you."

Then Nathanael declared, "Rabbi, you are the Son of God; you are the King of Israel."

Jesus said, "You believe because I told you I saw you under the fig-tree. You shall see greater things than that."

He then added, "I tell you the truth, you shall see heaven open, and the angels of God ascending and descending on the Son of Man."' Jesus prophesies directly into Nat's life. He lets him know that this unexpected encounter is set to become a vital relationship.

Supernatural Encounters

My mate's dad brought him up to believe that he was just a lump of meat spinning around on a rock and even though we sometimes sat up all night talking about God and the meaning of life, he can't shake off his atheistic upbringing. Strangely, I think he's the only true atheist that I've ever known. There's so much weird stuff around – UFOs, ETs, corn circles, ghosts, dreams, deja vues that most people guess there's 'something' out there, though very few of them have a way of defining or describing just what it is. Some can live with the uncertainty, some look for a scientific explanation and some just get freaked out. These days, though, few would be shy to admit that our lives are periodically interrupted by the supernatural. Currently, it's quite cool to be in touch with your spiritual side. People like the added enigma of suggesting that there is more to their persona than meets the eye.

I've had the privilege of travelling quite a lot, Niagara Falls, churning with deadly power and energy – the noise, the spray, the weird urge to jump in! The Great Barrier Reef, with its resident population of flamboyant fish, swimming towards you though the warm sea, curious and surprisingly confident. But how limited my descriptions are and how sad I would be if all my life revolved around a couple of experiences I had years ago! But some people do really live like that. Christians or not, it's an easy trap to fall into. The number of people who are dreaming that they're still going out with someone who dumped them months ago, still wearing combat trousers and pretending they're younger than they are. For the tribes we're reaching out to, our call is a call to let go of the past and have a supernatural encounter with God right here in the present, something personal and intimate between them and God, something that will show them in a moment what you couldn't explain in a lifetime! And the best bit is that it doesn't have to be a one off.

I've been a Christian for about seven years. No way do I know it all; in fact, most days, I think I know less than when I started. It's an adventure, a mystery to be solved. That's the way it's supposed to be. There is always an unexplainability with God – because he's God. If we can explain everything ourselves, what's the point of having a God? What distinguishes him from us? God declares of himself in Isaiah 55:8,9:

'"For my thoughts are not your thoughts, neither are your ways my ways,' declares the LORD. "As the heavens are higher than the earth, so are my ways higher than your ways and my thoughts than your thoughts."'

In the same way, what is the point of having faith if you only believe in the possible – what kind of faith is that?

'No eye has seen, no ear has heard, no mind has imagined what God has prepared for those who love him – but God has revealed it to us by his Spirit.' (1 Cor 2:9,10)

When I first told my mates that I'd accepted God into my life, they laughed their heads off – and a lot worse. Their general attitude was that I'd 'really lost it this time.' They said it wouldn't last. These are the same mates who were involved in the accidental riot I described in Chapter 2... I saw them all not long back at a stag do, in London. During the course of the day, which, incidentally, involved the most boring game of football I've ever seen, between Wimbledon and Derby County, they individually began to corner me for quiet little chats. One by one, they admitted to me that they were lost and looking for something. Later on that evening, sat on high bar stools outside a pub on Drury Lane, with a bit of Dutch courage inside them, they joined forces for a combined assault and asked me to describe what I knew about God. After talking for a while and getting nowhere, I pointed to a pint of beer. There was plenty around. All of us, I said, could try to reproduce that pint of beer. We could draw some diagrams, list the ingredients, talk about it; we'd probably even describe the same pint of beer differently but...

you've gotta taste it for yourself! Sadly, on that occasion, they chose to stick with the amber nectar rather than taste the water of life.

The fact remains that we are in the business of Total Christianity – the firm belief that what we talk about needs to be tasted. Jesus used a really clever example when he was having a secret late-night chat with a leading Jewish councillor who was struggling to get his head round all the mad stuff he was hearing.

Jesus answered, 'I tell you the truth, no one can enter the kingdom of God unless he is born of water and the Spirit. Flesh gives birth to flesh, but the Spirit gives birth to spirit. You should not be surprised at my saying, "You must be born again." The wind blows wherever it pleases. You hear its sound, but you cannot tell where it comes from or where it is going. So it is with everyone born of the Spirit.'

'How can this be?' Nicodemus asked.

'"You are Israel's teacher,' said Jesus, 'and do you not understand these things?

'I tell you the truth, we speak of what we know, and we testify to what we have seen, but still you people do not accept our testimony. I have spoken to you of earthly things and you do not believe; how then will you believe if I speak of heavenly things?' (John 3:5–12)

Pay attention to two key words there; no, not 'water' and 'spirit', but 'understand' and 'believe'. Jesus acknowledges Nick's quest for understanding but gently corrects him, stressing the importance of coming to a place of believing. There'll always be holes in our understanding, but you must encourage those around you to believe. Like Jesus here, I trust that you will find times when people come to you secretly, even – or especially – those who may have given you a really hard time publicly. Be alert. For those who God brings to you, those hidden moments could lead to major breakthroughs. What you believe is so important. That belief will become the thread in the needle of the Spirit which sews torn lives back together. That belief will take people beyond the encountering of God into a relationship with him.

chapter eight

The Right Packaging

I've not been married long, hence my Christmas gift tally notably included a tool kit, a magnetic telescopic and an illuminating screwdriver – just what every man needs! My sister gave me *The Matrix* on video. But I must confess that I took it back and swapped it for a PlayStation game – well, I have to stay in touch with youth culture, you see, and those games take hours to research properly! Sadly, last Christmas, I didn't tear off any wrapping paper and find any special surprises. There was nothing to think 'WOWWW' about. Call me ungrateful, I suppose, but then again, I didn't really ask for anything. There is a link between asking and getting. Funny, isn't it?

How about you? Did you ask for anything last Christmas? Did you get it? What about the previous year? Can you remember what you got? What about the year before that? It's so easy to get really greedy about things so temporary! Nothing lasts.

'You want what you don't have, so you scheme and kill to get it. You are jealous for what others have, and you can't possess it, so you fight and quarrel to take it away from them. And yet the reason is – you don't ask God for it. And even when you do ask, you don't get it because your whole motive is wrong. You want only what will give you pleasure.' (Jas 4:2,3)

So where is this going? A revealing question worth putting to people is:

'If I could give you anything you asked for, what would it be?'

Clearly, if you put that question to a broad sweep of people, you'd get a massive variety of answers. Think of the tribes who co-habit your world; how would they respond? There's the Townies – tracksuits, Rockport and H Samuel jewellery; the Moshers – black hoody, baggy pants and dangly chains; the Nerds – huddled around their computer mags; the Gangstas – covering up every part of their body bar the eye slits. This may not come as a shock to you but Jesus really is the fulfilment of every desire, the best gift anyone can receive, whatever tribe they belong to. Sadly, for years, he's only come in one kind of packaging – sandals and rainbow strap! He wants you to be his packaging to these tribes. That doesn't mean you have to go out and get a sudden image change but it is a challenge to push yourself out of any cultural comfort zones that you're hiding in. Imagine if the apostle Paul had limited himself to only reaching out to short, bald men!

These are still the early days of a new millennium – in case you hadn't noticed. Nothing much has changed, has it? Well, it's not going to change itself! Are you going to affect your world, and are you going to face it alone? As we wrap up this chapter on 'Tribes', let me make a suggestion. I suggest that we all make a deal together tonight! A deal between you, me and God! It's a deal that links right in with what I've just been on about – asking.

I don't know if you're into *Hillsongs*. I know they've not quite got *The Tribe's* musical cutting edge but they do write great songs, even if some of them sound as if they belong on 80s movie soundtracks! One song that I often blast up to neighbour-annoying volumes is called 'You said'. It quotes the promise of God from Psalm 2, *'Ask of me, and I will make the nations your inheritance, the ends of the earth your possession.'*

That's what I'd like you to agree with me and God here and now. That you'll begin to claim those tribes for Jesus in prayer. Allow God to drop in your mind an image of those he wants you to reach.

'Ask, and God will give to you. Search, and you will find. Knock, and the door will open for you. Yes, everyone who asks will receive. Everyone who searches will find. And everyone who knocks will have the door opened.' (Matt 7:7,8)

chapter eight

chapter nine

led to the lost

The greater the gift costs the giver,
and the less the recipient deserves it,
the greater the love is seen to be.
Measured by these standards, God's love
in Christ is absolutely unique.

Following Instructions

A city banker is travelling to a business conference at a country hotel. Utterly lost on the winding single-track roads, he stops to ask a farmer. The farmer leans through the electrically operated window into the pristine leather interior and politely listens to the exasperated gentleman before obliging with:

'Take your first left by the oak tree and follow this road all the way by the barley field. Left again at the gate, keep left over the cattle grid and left by the rusty gate.'

The driver zooms off but in five minutes time, finds himself in exactly the same spot. He sees the farmer again and screeches to a halt, furious.

'What do you think you're playing at?' He screams.

The farmer looks back very calmly, clears his throat and explains:

'Well you see, the way to the hotel is quite complicated – I needed to know that you could follow some simple instructions.'

This chapter is a reflection on the simple signposts which God offers us in his word to ensure that when we find ourselves touring the back alleys of human emotions, we will know the way forward.

A Caring People

Around the *Message* office, I've earned the tag, 'Matt "caring" Wilson', after St Paul the Caring! Before you think I'm serious, let's stop there. Clearly it was after St Paul the 'explain "tact" to me one more time, please, Barnabas'. The great gung-ho Apostle, whizzing here and there, launching gospel salvos at unsuspecting Gentiles; being so offensive that he was on the receiving end of regular battering; circumcising poor Timothy in his late teens – *ouch*! Let's look at Paul's journey, not just in miles but also in personal growth as God forms character in him on his travels.

Taking a fast forward scan of Acts from chapter 15, we see that Paul falls out with his top mate Barnabas and sets off with Silas through what is now Lebanon and Turkey. He picks up Timothy in Lystra. Soon after that, he dreams about a man calling him from the region of Macedonia (near Istanbul). Off they go, dropping off Luke in Philippi after the miraculous jail-break. Eventually, the great traveller ends up in Thessalonica, to a less-than-warm reception.

'These men that have turned the world upside down have come hither also.'
(Acts 17:6)

Because Luke, the writer of Acts, stops off in Philippi, a renowned medical centre, the order and specific details of Paul's later movements have only a minimal recording in Acts. So let's pick them up in Paul's own words, recounted in 1 Thessalonians 2:7–12.

'As apostles of Christ, we could have been a burden to you, but we were gentle among you, like a mother caring for her little children. We loved you so much that we were delighted to share with you not only the gospel of God but our lives as well, because you had become so dear to us. Surely you remember, brothers, our toil and hardship; we worked night and day in order not to be a burden to anyone while we preached the gospel of God to you. You are witnesses, and so is God, of how holy, righteous and blameless we were among you who believed. For you know that we dealt with each of you as a father deals with his own children, encouraging, comforting and urging you to live lives worthy of God, who calls you into his kingdom and glory.'

Family Photos

The first thing we notice here is the way Paul used the images of family while talking to the church in Thessalonica. He must have sat down to write, his head full of faces and memories. They didn't have photo albums in ancient Greece but I can just imagine him unwrapping a dog-eared piece of paper from his little box of personal belongings and looking at a childish sketch of a short, bald man with the title, 'Uncle Paul'. He'd remember fathers, mothers, children. So much emotion.

The church there was pretty young and we gather that it had a real family feel. Unlike many other towns and cities which he passed through at lightning speed, Paul slowed down there. He settled for a while, got a job and met up with the local people in his spare time.

My mum has an old Bible with the original Greek text. I go round and borrow it when I want to get below the surface of the words, to experience the feelings and the intimacy. It's wonderful. Except that I can't actually read Greek! So I go round to spend some time with a gorgeous Greek family who are part of my church. Like all the Greeks I've ever met, they're superb hosts. I feel so welcome and at home. They give me Greek cake and we sit squashed in the back room with mum and grown-up kids. On one occasion we looked at this passage together in the original ancient language, they told me of the powerful love being expressed in these verses.

The 'mother' word in verse 7 actually means a foster-mother, not a natural mother. The whole meaning is that of growing to love the children as their own. Other versions describe this by using the word 'nurse' or 'nursing mother'. In those days, if the real mother was for any reason unable to look after her baby, it was customary for a family friend to help. Often the foster-mum would become so attached to the child that she'd have difficulty in letting go again. That's the process that Paul felt as he loved these Christians through their formative early years. There are three real highlights in the piece:

1. The caring feeling is not a straightforward 'nanny' emotion – it was described to me as a 'warm love, heat like the sun, love with temperature'.
2. It's more than normal family affection – they showed me the *agapetos* connection hiding behind the understated 'dear to us'. Agape is a word with 'covenant' and 'kingdom' connection. It's used for example in Colossians 1:13 *'...he has rescued us from the kingdom of darkness and brought us into the kingdom of the Son he loves...'*
3. It didn't happen overnight – apparently the word for *'become'*, in *'become so dear to us'* is telling of a drawn-out and troublesome birth.

Do you get it? We're into the juicy stuff now! Paul is revealing to us the role of the evangelist in the maturing process of a growing body of believers, the Ephesians 4 connection. Odd-shaped people thrown together as a strange foster-family. Mums, dads, teenagers, kids, all the time new additions. Noise, laughter, tears, fall-outs! But growing together in unity of faith, reaching the promised measure of fulness in Christ. Let's allow ourselves to be like Paul. Drawn into this painful caring process and developing this love with temperature. You get the impression that during their time together, the person who changed the most was Paul, the evangelist among them! Have I mentioned that before?

chapter nine

The 'Yes Yes's' and The 'No No's'

1 Thessalonians chapter 2

YES YES	NO NO
Encouragement v12	Flattery v5
Comfort v12	Cover up v5
Godly lifestyle v12	Glory hunting v6
His kingdom and glory v12	My ministry and recognition v6

All of us, without exception, no matter how 'sorted' we think we are, should be willing to change. If the apostle Paul could, we can, too. We are all what we are, yet all the time dying to ourselves to become something new. However painful the process, we change into a lover and a carer in the family of God. God takes great pleasure in transforming lives, and our surrender to him is worship in every sense.

I can feel a bit of a detour coming on…

Led by Worship – Mike Pilavachi

I don't want to reduce worship to slushy romanticism; it's so much more than that. There is an element of adoration and intimacy, even of affection in the right sense, which is meant to happen in our worship. At *Soul Survivor*, we're totally sold on that. However, we've realised something recently. We've noticed how worship has been compartmentalised. Worship has been kept in the church and kept separate from evangelism. Worship is done in the church and evangelism is done out there in the world. We've been asking, 'Where did that come from?' because it doesn't come from the Bible!

Some of us, we're into the worship stuff and that's basically all we do. Others of us, we're into evangelism; we go out there telling everyone, and it can be hard work!

'Oh no, I've got to do the E-word! I've got to go and I've got to tell everyone and give leaflets out on Saturday afternoon and sing songs in front of everyone. I'm gonna die. I've gotta do this mime, oh, my goodness. I've gotta do it coz he saved me and I've gotta pay him back.'

And it's all out of duty. Do you know that the best evangelism is the evangelism that flows out of worship? And the only real worship is the worship that flows into

True worship is the expression of a love relationship.

evangelism. They belong together; they were never meant to be separated.

True worship is the expression of a love relationship. It's like when Matt Redman was falling in love with Beth, he talked about her continually. You couldn't get him off the subject. No one said to him,

'Now you've met Beth, it's your duty to tell everyone about her. You really must. Why don't you give out some leaflets about her?'

No one said that! Talking about Beth was an overflow of his love. And the best evangelism, the only evangelism that is long term effective is the evangelism which issues out of a love relationship with Jesus. When you see him and fall in love with him, you're immersed in God, and you can't help it. You end up talking about him wherever you go.

Fixing the Co-ordinates of your Destiny

Life is made up of combinations of moments and places. You can be in the right place, but at the wrong time. Lots of times during my Uni days, I'd end up coming home from my job at the Student Union bar at three in the morning. As if that wasn't bad enough, there was absolutely no way of predicting when the night bus was going to roll along.

Often I'd stand pointlessly at the bus stop – *right place, wrong time*.

Of course, you can be on time at the wrong place. When I was trying to initiate *M2K* projects in Macclesfield, I was getting really annoyed standing outside an office waiting for someone – only to find out later that he'd been waiting at my office.

I'm trying to reduce the number of occasions when I find myself at the wrong place at the wrong time. Now and again I get myself to the right place – at the right time! I have a vivid memory of doing detached work in Wythenshawe on a scorching hot day. Together with some of the guys and girls from our detached youth work team, I'd decided to get out in the sun, on the park, meet some kids and have a good, safe time. As we mooched around all the regular haunts, we found absolutely nobody. Had the scary child catcher from *Chitty Chitty Bang*

Bang rounded them all up? We had to find out. Our first lead was a lone child sitting on a squeaky swing. Trying not to look too scary, we ambled over and launched into our youth-worker-style-greeting routine.

'Yo – Yo, check, check, one, no doubt.' (Not really.)

We did find out some useful information, though. Apparently, everyone who was anyone had gone to a legendary hang-out called 'Red Rock'. Between us, we hadn't a clue what or where it was, but we would find out.

Half an hour and numerous phone calls later, we pulled up in the car just around the corner from the location that had been described to us. It was a weir in a dirty stretch of river round the back of a derelict old mill. Kids were everywhere – on the grass, in the water, in the trees, hundreds of them. It was detached youthwork heaven! It quickly became clear to us that something was not quite right. The situation was that we were on 'the dark side', in the shade of the trees. It was the other side of the river, the side drenched in blazing sunlight, that had all the kids. As we shuffled closer along the high bank, a lad on the other side recognised me.

'Hey, Matt, are y' coming in?'

With that, he jumped into the foaming water, narrowly avoiding a shopping trolley which was clearly a long way from home. Another young lad followed right after him, zooming off the six foot bank on his bike! A few more lads spotted us and began to holler over the water. We were clearly at a point of decision. To make matters worse, I still had a talk rattling round my head that I'd presented to some churches, the title 'Bridge Building Youth Work'. Did we need a bridge now! I looked at my mate Tim, we both turned and looked at the two girls accompanying us. They shook their heads disapprovingly. All eyes were fixed on us now. It was as if the future credibility of our work with this group of young people hung in the balance. Without another thought, we pulled off our T-shirts and jumped...

From that day on, the dynamic of our relationship with that group of un-reachable young people totally changed. They became open to us for all kinds of positive input in their lives. God had made sure that we were in the right place at the right time. That young lad who knew my name had provided the link we needed or else, to be honest, we might have bottled out. The world in which God has created a destiny for us is made of so much more than time and space – the world is full of people. God wants to position each one of us to fulfil our destiny and that position is measured by places, times and relationships.

PLACE + TIME + RELATIONSHIP = POSITION

With all the random directions the forces of life can spin us in, it's a wonder we find our way to the lost, the endless permutations! In many ways, simply navigating moments and places can become a bit of a merry-go-round; when people are in the equation, just watch the God action really kick in.

Let's look at some people God has used significantly throughout history. Each had a time, a place and a relationship which completed the right position for God's plan to unfold. It'll all become clear to you along the way.

We'll start with Joseph. The bulk of material on him is found at the back end of Genesis. I'd like to quote from chapter 41:9 onwards.

'Then the chief cupbearer said to Pharaoh,

"Today I am reminded of my shortcomings. Pharaoh was once angry with his servants, and he imprisoned me and the chief baker in the house of the captain of the guard. Each of us had a dream the same night, and each dream had a meaning of its own. Now a young Hebrew was there with us, a servant of the captain of the guard. We told him our dreams, and he interpreted them for us, giving each man the interpretation of his dream. And things turned out exactly as he interpreted them to us: I was restored to my position, and the other man was hanged."

So Pharaoh sent for Joseph, and he was quickly brought from the dungeon. When he had shaved and changed his clothes, he came before Pharaoh.'

Joseph found himself positioned by God. He was called out of obscurity at the threshold of a time of severe social and economic trial throughout the known world. His rapid promotion to high position initiated a purpose which saved their civilisation. God is working in your life with the same principles, positioning you for purpose.

Secondly, Daniel's story, which proves once again that there is more to our position than our external circumstances. As a captive in a foreign land, he had every reason to grumble and protest, to allow himself to slacken off and even sink into depression. Unsurprisingly, God planned to use Daniel's position to bring great glory to God himself. The co-ordinates of his destiny were Babylon, at the time of the exile of Judah, with a man you may not have heard of before – Arioch.

'When Arioch, the commander of the king's guard, had gone out to put to *death the wise men of Babylon, Daniel spoke to him with wisdom and tact. He asked the king's officer, "Why did the king issue such a harsh decree?"*

Arioch then explained the matter to Daniel.' (Dan 2:14,15)

Between the lines of this brief snippet of dialogue we can sense the exchange taking place between these two men. Something clearly clicks. The guy turns up with an order to kill Daniel, along with all his mates. Instead, they get into conversation and he even begins to question the orders he's received from the king himself. Let's read on:

'Then Daniel went to Arioch, whom the king had appointed to execute the wise men of Babylon, and said to him, "Do not execute the wise men of Babylon. Take me to the king, and I will interpret his dream for him." Arioch took Daniel to the king at once and said, "I have found a man among the exiles from Judah who can tell the king what his dream means." The king asked Daniel (also called Belteshazzar), "Are you able to tell me what I saw in my dream and interpret it?" Daniel replied, "No wise man, enchanter, magician or diviner can explain to the king the mystery he has asked about, but there is a God in heaven who reveals mysteries. He has shown King Nebuchadnezzar what will happen in days to come. Your dream and the visions that passed through your mind as you lay on your bed are these..." (Dan 2:24–28).

And Daniel goes on to describe the secrets of the King's mind as if it were his own. That single act so moved the King that he made Daniel and his associates the most powerful men in the empire. Essentially, what God was doing amounted to a positioning for presence right at the heart of that vast power system. In seeing the world come to a knowledge of his glory, God will position people for presence close to those of influence. You might never get to be adviser to King Charles but that's no great loss. He may well need you to bring his presence into your Uni or office alongside key tutors or managers.

Finally, we come to Peter, hiding in the post-ascension shadows, still sweating it out in Jerusalem, trying to make sense of the Messiah's promises hanging over his life. Suddenly, as Peter sits praying in a room with his mates, God arrives in the fiery shape of the Holy Spirit. Before he knows what's hit him, Peter's out in the street, getting blank looks from several thousand bewildered people. Words are tumbling out of his mouth, *'Fellow Jews...'*

The first thing the Holy Spirit inspires him to do is to affirm his relationship with those who are listening. The timing is important, the place is significant and the relationship is vital. In the eternal plan of God, this is positioning for power.

How we need the power of God to be demonstrated in and through our lives! What good are our wise words without the Spirit's power? What can we do in our own strength that will make any lasting impact on the hearts of the people we meet?

It's time for the new generation of evangelists to get into position. If you don't know where to start, then consider this.

'And God raised us up with Christ and seated us with him in the heavenly realms in Christ Jesus, in order that in the coming ages, he might show the incomparable riches of his grace, expressed in his kindness to us in Christ Jesus' (Eph 2:6,7).

On *Xcelerate*, we have to put a stop to false humility. It can really get you trapped. In the heavenly realm, you're already in a position of perfection. We are encouraged in the word to meditate on our position in Christ.

'Since, then, you have been raised with Christ, set your hearts on things above, where Christ is seated at the right hand of God. Set your minds on things above, not on earthly things,' (Col 3:1–2).

The *New Living Bible* says, *'Set your minds on the realities of heaven!'*

Now, from this new perspective, let's allow ourselves to be led to the lost. It's not a random, drifting backpacker kind of leading but a deliberate God-initiated positioning in the place that we can affect the most lives with God's love.

Ponder on this little equation before you start the next chapter.

   POSITION
+ PURPOSE
+ PRESENCE
+ POWER
= DESTINY

chapter ten

sent out

Do all the good you can,
by all the means you can,
in all the ways you can,
in all the places you can,
at all the times you can,
to all the people you can,
as long as ever you can.

John Wesley

Initiative

It's quite easy to talk about new 'initiatives' as though we're doing God a favour. Like he's sat there stuck for ideas and we need to loosen up that old grey matter for him. What a massive misconception! This is God who, from his endless resources of creativity, spun the entire universe into being. This is Jesus who sustains all things by his powerful word, our commissioning King, our sending Saviour.

He gives clear instructions to his twelve main men in Matthew chapter 10, specifying where to go and where to avoid, what to say and what not to say, what to take and what to leave at home. He is the master strategist who knows exactly how to get the job done. To our limited human intellects, his plans don't always make sense at first, such as marching round a city seven times! Yet as we obey him, time and again, we're stunned by what he can achieve through us. In John chapter 17 he prays to his Father, '...as you sent me into the world, I have sent them into the world.' The Greek word used here is *apostello* – sound familiar? It's where we get the term Apostle; the twelve disciples became the Apostles, 'the sent ones'. *Apostello* crops up all over the place in the New Testament as 'the sent ones' spread the good news throughout the world.

'When the apostles in Jerusalem heard that Samaria had accepted the word of God, they sent [apostello] Peter and John to them' (Acts 8:14).

Paul himself received a personal sending from Jesus on his ill-fated journey to Damascus, which he recounts in Acts 26:12 and goes on to explain in Romans 10:14,15.

'...how can they believe in the one of whom they have not heard? And how can they hear without someone preaching to them? And how can they preach unless they are sent [apostello]?'

Jesus left one final word ringing in the ears of his disciples. That word was 'Go!', the great commission. Throughout the next few pages, we'll be working out the when, where and how of this great sending. I've asked trailblazing evangelist Mark Ritchie to kick us off.

chapter ten
The Cage

A few years ago, I was invited to take a team of young people down to Belvedere in South East London. The team was part of *Flamethrowers* – a youth missions programme I head up. In the team, there was a real mix of people of different ages and experiences. I was particularly conscious that we had a few fifteen-year-old girls on the team.

Once we hit the ground, one of the first things we did was a bit of exploring, searching for the best places to connect with young people in the area. Asking a few leading questions, we found out about 'the cage'. The cage was a basketball court with huge wire fences around it, hemmed in by blocks of high-rise flats, with loads of mess and graffiti everywhere. It was a gloomy, fearful place and the evenings brought a greater shadow in this hole carved out of the ground. There was a pervading rather chilling feeling, but it wasn't anything to do with the weather.

The local youth leader told me the story of a recent knifing which didn't ease my mood in any way! The crunch came when I asked the local leader straight out, 'Would you allow your church youth group to go into the cage to chat to these local kids?' He thought for a moment and said, 'No; what if something happened?'

I didn't sleep well that night, as I was torn between seeing the desperation amongst the lost youths messing around in the cage and being a responsible mission leader. Thoughts came pouring into my mind. What if something happened to one of those lovely Christian fifteen-year-old girls? What would I say to her parents? I felt God speaking into my spirit, 'Greater is he that is in you, than he that is in the world.'

The next day, we went down to the cage. The team was amazing, chatting and mixing with these gangs. I felt incredibly uneasy at the amount of attention some of these gang lads were giving one or two of the young girls in my team. Some of the provocative and sexual language they were using around and towards them concerned me. I stood in the cage, praying silently: the whole time, I was totally on edge yet at the end of the first day, the team members were so encouraged by the gang's response that they all wanted to go back.

I didn't relax fully on any of the trips to the cage and one incident nearly swayed me to give up on the cage idea altogether. My whole team was in there playing basketball, building relationships, when a youth climbed down the fence and started shouting crazily. All the youths from the cage were panicking and running, and in the low, dark, gloomy place, fear was everywhere. The news which the lad spread was of another gang on the way, looking for trouble. I got my team into the minibus as quickly as I could. Some of my team felt I had over-reacted and maybe fear won in my heart that day. It's funny that it was the younger ones I was trying to protect, like the young girl from Tunbridge Wells, who gave me the most grief about leaving.

We went back later and as the week progressed, I gripped tighter and tighter that word God had given me. Incredibly, the relationships between my *Flamethrowers* team and those teenagers grew and grew. On the Friday, we invited them to an event at the church. The whole gang came, and when the gospel was preached, Billy, the gang leader, responded. As he came to the front, many of us just cried. I will never forget the emotion of our team; many of them wept and laughed. At the end of the evening, I wrote in my journal, 'Thank you God! I have been scared, tired, upset and emotional and you have been there every step of the way.' My courage came and went, but ultimately, God never went anywhere; he was with me the whole time.

Pioneers Need Partners

Thinking about 'sending', we need to talk about Dynamic Duos. They're everywhere. There's the archetypal Batman and Robin, Buzz Lightyear & Woody; Richard & Judy; Ant & Dec. What about Bible equivalents?

Moses and Aaron, Joshua and Caleb, Jonathan and his Armourbearer – now they were quite a pair. Jonathan, heir to the throne, gets fed up with all the stick his people are taking. He comes up with a harebrained plan to take on the enemy nation single-handed. The young lad who looks after his military wardrobe is on the spot and comes out with one of the most encouraging lines in the whole of the Bible.

'Do all that you have in mind,' his armour-bearer said. *'Go ahead; I am with you heart and soul'* (1 Sam 14:7).

I've heard it said that everybody needs an armour-bearer and everybody needs to be an armour-bearer. When you're taking the message behind enemy lines, you need someone watching your back. But you need to be looking out for those around you, too. Jonathan wasn't a walking disaster zone who needed someone sweeping up after him wherever he went; he was just as sharp in spirit. The heart shown towards him by his armour-bearer he reflects to his covenant friend, David.

'Jonathan said to David, "Whatever you want me to do, I'll do for you"' (1 Sam 20:4).

As we read on through history, we see the great achievements of Ezra and Nehemiah, restoring the city of Jerusalem, first the temple then the walls. Daniel hand-picks his partners in the cause and God proves himself to a pagan nation. We hit the New Testament and find the dynamic duos ensuring the working out of God's will. Mary and Mary carrying the amazing news of the resurrection in Matthew 28, Peter and John testifying to the Sanhedrin in Acts 4:19.

'Judge for yourselves whether it is right in God's sight to obey you rather than God. For we cannot help speaking about what we have seen and heard.'

Paul, with Barnabas, Silas and Timothy. It's plain to see that on many, many occasions, major forward leaps in the working out of God's plans are made by partnerships and teams, clusters of people of synchronised spirit and purpose, released into the world to win ground-breaking successes for King Jesus. He is in the business of bringing together people whose joining creates a unit stronger than the sum of its parts. There are some anointed loners in the Bible, your Jeremiahs, Ezekiels and John the Baptists, but note, they're mostly prophets and usually weird!

Jesus was the ultimate team-builder. With just twelve young men and a few dedicated women, he turned the world upside down. The book of Acts records just how, after his ascension, that team began to grow and affect the world. Jesus' personal appearance on the road to Damascus to recruit Paul was to be the signing of the season! Paul acknowledged that his ministry was not complete without his 'partners in the gospel'. People who he 'ran the race' with. I know what he's getting at there because although I now find it hard to believe, once upon a time, I actually ran a marathon!

It was all God's fault. For months, he'd been growing a vision inside me of

Manchester totally on fire for him, every house in every street becoming a place of prayer and worship, lives being turned around, real revival stuff. This all coincided with Andy offering me the job of kick-starting the *Message 2000* concept. Someone had given me a prophetic picture in which I was running and each footprint was blazing with fire. I thought that picture was pretty cool. On top of all this, I was being stirred up by that verse from Joshua; 'Every place you set your foot will be yours.' The stage was set for some radical action. Then I saw it, a feature in the paper, 'Manchester Marathon 1998 – apply now'. I had no choice. It felt like destiny, except that I'd not run anywhere for about six years!

It was all God's fault. For months, he'd been growing a vision inside me of Manchester totally on fire for him.

Serious training began and my daily prayer walks became prayer jog. To be honest, it was one of the most spiritually alert times I've ever known in my life but I was dying on my feet. Each step was a prayer but not always for the lost; it was more like, 'Father, if this cup can be taken from me…'. Trust me, marathon training is no picnic. I tried to recruit myself some pace-setters but strangely enough, nobody was particularly interested in accompanying me on soggy circuits of Wythenshawe Park. To be honest, with a week to go, I think I would've jacked it all in but for the constant encouragement of my mum.

I arrived at the start area in Heaton Park early in the morning and gave all the necessary bits and bobs the Vaseline treatment. Wouldn't want twenty-six miles with jogger's nipple, after all. As I was limbering up, I heard a chirpy 'Hello, Matt.' It was one of the crew from *Planet Life*, a burly fireman called Bob, veteran marathon runner and really nice bloke, too. As he began to explain his strategy for breaking the five-hour barrier, I realised how unprepared I was. I started making all kinds of excuses about my dodgy knees and new shoes.

'Stick with me, son,' said Bob, 'You'll be fine.' And you know what, I was. He paced me, coached me and encouraged me for the first seventeen miles until he was sure that I was going to make it, then he shot off and I didn't see him again until the finish line!

As I survey this twenty-first century landscape that we find ourselves in I can only see one way forward. Evangelists young and old coming together in clusters and pairs, a purposeful, anointed unity that we've not experienced before. These Pioneering partnerships are essential to God's strategic breakthrough into the consciousness of many currently oblivious neighbourhoods in and around this nation.

The Unsung Heroes

I want us to spend a little more time looking at the apostle Paul. Can we learn anything from his methods, and more importantly, can we learn anything from his relationships? How many of you have heard of Tertius? You should have. Without him, it's unlikely that we'd have the most awesome exposition of Christian doctrine available, the book of Romans. Tertius wrote it down. What about Sosthenes, Paul's Corinthian friend who took a beating for him on at least one occasion? Epaphroditus, whom Paul describes in his letter to the Philippians as, '…brother, fellow worker and fellow soldier…'. There's the vertically-challenged Tychicus, who appears throughout Paul's writings as a trusted encourager of the saints, willing to travel great journeys to carry the cause.

Open your Bible and take a look at the Romans 16 posse, the personal remarks which make the letter so much more meaningful. I get upset when people wrongly interpret the letters of Paul, projecting the clearly written authority back onto his personality, thus creating a distorted image of a dogmatic, authoritarian chauvinist. Come on, read them again; that image could not be further from the truth. Paul found it quite natural to form strong and purposeful friendships with a fantastic diversity of people. They were of many nationalities; some were slaves, others rich and powerful. Out of the list of twenty-six friends in Romans 16, nine are women!

The Key Three

In Paul's life and ministry, there were three really key partners in the gospel. Firstly, Barnabas; he made the initial and seriously risky alliance with Paul. Let's not forget that Paul was responsible for the imprisonment and cold-blooded murder of Barny's mates.

Barnabas has a good rep. He is an early member of the church community. The two meet in Acts chapter 9. Barnabas sees something which the other believers, blinded by their fears and preconceptions, can't see. He takes Paul to the Apostles. He has everything to lose! Fortunately for us all, they make the right call and Paul is accepted, but, as will become the pattern of his ministry, trouble follows him! You don't have to read many verses before you find him causing commotion and receiving death threats. The boys send him home to Tarsus and things cool down a bit.

On his next assignment, Antioch, just a short boat ride from Tarsus, Barnabas goes off to find Paul, determined to see him released into his ministry. He can't bear to think of that locked-up potential so he recruits him as the first team member in the place where the name 'Christian' was invented. He sticks with Paul until he is established and can take full leadership, although he keeps him a safe distance from the establishment in Jerusalem!

Switch to Acts 15:36; clearly time has passed and the relationship has hit a crisis point. Barnabas is wanting to take another risky character, Mark, aka John Mark, on the next trip, Paul disagrees. In steps Silas, a leader from the Jerusalem hierachy. Not simply a 'silent partner' or a bag carrier, he's his own man.

He was a prophet who said much to encourage and strengthen... (Acts 15:32)

He preaches powerfully, according to 2 Corinthians 1:19. He becomes an inseparable unit with Paul in the travels detailed in Acts chapters 15, 16 and 17, Paul and Barnabas are hardly ever mentioned except together. They even share beatings and jail cells; yes, singing in jail! What a picture of *Pioneering Partnership!* Together they pioneer churches in many major Gentile towns and cities. Here's the important note, though; they don't become an exclusive unit. When they meet Timothy in Lystra (Acts chapter 16), there is room for him to join.

So we welcome Timothy, a partner from a different generation. I like the fact that he shows the faith to go beyond his physical weakness. He shows the spirit to seize the day; when invited by Paul to join the team, he doesn't dither around for a fortnight. No, he's a guy who seizes an opportunity. This young guy becomes indispensable to a well-established missionary unit. He is prepared completely to leave behind his ordinary sphere and go to new places. As we read the letters sent to him by Paul years later, we find out that he never lets the dust settle on him but keeps on moving. In those letters, we find a lot of church doctrine but again, it's the personal remarks which hit the spot. Have a look at 2 Timothy 4:9–19; this is where we get our third insight into the qualities of pioneering partnerships. Paul values the person over the project. Let's sum that up then, the lessons to be learnt from Paul's key three, three qualities of a pioneering partner:

1. Take a risk to release
2. Don't become exclusive
3. Value the person

Never Walk Alone

As *Xcelerate* has developed, the 'dynamic duo', Colette and I, needed to grow to become a 't'riffic trio'. We scoured the world for the right person and not for the first time, God pointed us to someone right under our noses. Here he is – globe-trotting Steve Graham will wrap up this chapter.

Possibly the best part of the 'being sent' process is the knowledge that however alone you feel, you're not! At the time of setting off, it's easy to think that it won't be too much of a problem to go it alone; after all, we've been commissioned! If only it were so simple! Out there in the field, it doesn't take long to figure out that the echoing words of our commissioning can be great, but we can't do without minute-by-minute help from the main man.

In August 2000, my home church sent me out to Thailand. In my mind, I was leaving on a single-handed mission for God to transform this Buddhist nation into a God-fearing society. I had nothing more than a plane ticket, a picture of the place I was heading for and a couple of names and addresses. Getting there was no problem but it took me a while to get acclimatised, getting used to the lack of any hot water while beginning to teach at the Bible school. God showed he was there; people were being saved, new leaders were being raised up, local orphans were being rescued and things were looking good.

Then came the Jungle. Forty-five degrees in the shade, a machete, a piece of canvas and a group of naïve students under my leadership, sent off to tell the natives about God. The easy part was getting their attention; after all, they'd never seen anyone with white skin before! Getting them to accept Jesus was the major challenge. Particularly hard was persuading them that he couldn't just be added to their random collection of gods. The fact that there is only one God, but that he's part of a Trinity, is not an easy concept to explain through two interpreters. Mentally, it was a real challenge – but we had been sent.

The folks at home were praying, the Bible college was praying, and we were not alone. We knew as never before that we needed the Holy Spirit and thankfully, we felt him with us. In a fresh way, we realised why Jesus encouraged the disciples to wait until they received the Helper. It was only through his power that we saw these people reached, new churches established and even witch-doctors set free from years of torment so that they could live for the one true God.

'Being sent' doesn't mean that God stands and waves until he can't see you. He is always with you.

chapter
ten

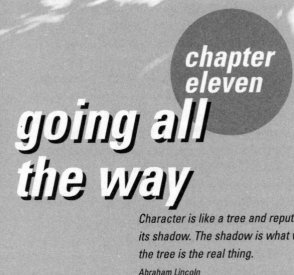

going all
the way

*Character is like a tree and reputation like
its shadow. The shadow is what we think of it;
the tree is the real thing.*
Abraham Lincoln

Success?

If you've managed to get this far through the book, then you must have gathered that the life story of an evangelist is not one of numerous overnight successes. 'Success' only comes before 'work' in the dictionary. This chapter is dedicated to keeping your heart beating as you fulfil all the demands of your commission. I've asked Colette Smethurst, the real hero of the *Xcelerate* leadership team, to kick us off here.

When I moved to Wythenshawe nearly five years ago, I thought revival was going to be along in about two to three weeks, maybe a month 'if the Lord tarries'! After all, with the arrival of thirty radical, relevant, spirit-filled Christians on the estate, who wasn't going to want to be a Christian! Since then, I've been suitably humbled but I've also learnt some massive lessons, mainly about faithfulness and perseverance – God's abundant supply and my desperate need for it!

Over the last five years, our work in Wythenshawe has been a process of building relationships with the young people and their families, and for me that has revolved predominantly around a small group of girls.

I first met them when they came to the youth club we ran. They were well feisty and I remember being a bit intimidated by them, even though they were only twelve, but over that first year, we witnessed God softening their tough exteriors and a year later, most of them had become Christians. They're all now part of the youth cell I lead with my husband. It's an adventurous and unpredictable journey that we travel with these girls; it can sometimes be discouraging and frustrating, and I often wish it weren't so messy, but I've seen God's faithfulness so we persevere.

At the moment, the scene is looking pretty good. One of the girls we've known for the last four years, who has shown us constant discouragement and apathy, told me last week that she was a Christian. Only six months ago she was anti-God, anti-Church and often anti-us… she's leading cell next week! Another girl who hasn't been to cell for weeks just turned up at church on Sunday; another was telling me how she has been reading her Bible, and about how her bag had been nicked and she needed to find out about enemies and forgiveness. One week, they brought a friend and the following week, she came and prayed out loud for the first time; you learn to celebrate even the smallest victories because you never know when you may turn the corner and see something not so good!

chapter eleven

And so here we are in Wythenshawe, nearly five years on. We have about thirty young people in cells, over forty in the youth club and every day, our schools team 'sows seeds' to hundreds more. It's not full-blown revival yet but if Abraham could wait twenty-five years for a son, if the Israelites could wait forty years for the promised land, if Noah could wait one hundred years for rain, then maybe we'll persevere a bit longer!

God's Timing

For a few crazy years in my late teens, I lived by the motto:

'Live fast, die young, leave a good-looking corpse.'

After several miraculous scrapes in some seriously hairy situations, I really did begin to think that I was invincible. Maybe I was part Mysteron like Captain Scarlet! In the wee small hours of a very rainy night in early September, my mate and I were cruising home from a club with a couple of lovely ladies in the car. Bless 'em, they'd just got back safely from a month's inter-railing in Europe. Then they got into a car with me. Well, of course they did, it was the passion-wagon, after all! Who wouldn't want to have a spin around the countryside in a pea green Vauxhall Cavalier Estate? Yeah, baby! Of course, like every self-respecting boy racer, I had the music pumping, heads were nodding, the speed was climbing, the bend was approaching, the bend was approaching...

...THE BEND IS APPROACHING! The girl in the passenger seat screams as I try to take control of the skidding car. In a fancy bit of Colin McRae action, I flick the back end into line but we're still travelling way too fast on the wrong side of the road and the wheels are locking up on me. Suddenly, the road twists back on itself. Way before I have any chance to compensate, we clip the verge and crash mercilessly into a low wall. The impact demolishes the loose stones and with almost scripted accuracy, the car mounts the wall like a monorail line, all four wheels completely off the ground. On the other side of the wall is total blackness and we are tilting closer and closer to it, still hurtling down this stony tramline. It's all going too fast, my foot is rammed on the brakes but of course nothing is happening. I see something coming straight for us like a bullet; , wood splits and metal screams but we come to an instant halt. Slow motion becomes heavy breathing. We're stationary. We're saved. I look around and we're all there, apparently alive. Saved by the tree. A very clever, self-sacrificing tree, might I add.

If a tree was ever in the right place at the right time, then it was this one.

My mate in the back seat was the first to make a move. After uttering a string of expletives, he swung his door open and stepped out. The next thing we heard through the eerie silence was a splash. We were hanging about six feet over a brook. There is no doubt in my mind that but for our friendly tree, we'd have been in it, upside down, without much chance of getting back out. We were saved in the middle of a very mad situation. Every one of us had been thinking ' ...this is it!'

Then the tree! Not a very big tree. But enough of a tree to stop us dead. A split second later and I would not be telling you this story. And if there's one thing that God knows about, it's split seconds. He's always right on time.

You see, at just the right time, when we were still powerless, Christ died for the ungodly. (Rom 5:6)

God has a habit of turning up at just the right time. Not a minute too early, not a minute too late. He shows us in the Bible, just as we see in life, that there are two kinds of time. There is the day to day plod and there is 'time within time' – special moments of opportunity, Seconds seem like hours and hours seem like seconds... It's like when England played Greece in that crucial World Cup qualifier. England were losing 1-0 and Sven decided to bring on Sheringham. With his first touch of the ball, he headed it in. He was on the pitch at just the right time. Then later in the game, in injury time, Beckham stepped up and scored the goal that put England through to the World Cup. I know that at that moment, my clock seemed to have stopped. I was sharing a moment with millions of people. Life has moments like that; when they happen, I get a bit goose-bumpy and start thinking, 'Hey, God, what are you up to?'

I think that's what this bit of the Bible is about – at just the right time, Christ died... It's not saying that Friday afternoon in Jerusalem, almost 2,000 years ago, was the right time; no, there's something deeper than that. I can close my eyes now and it's like yesterday to me, pictures from the Bible before my eyes... The sky goes black as night for three hours but it's midday, and it's not an eclipse. The earth shakes – rocks split and dead people wake up! An eternal moment breaks into time when Christ says, ' It is finished!'

Pay attention to the experience that Colette has told you about. It may not happen to you overnight. In your own mission to see the people around you won for Christ, try to remember that it will happen according to God's appointments. He doesn't work to calendars with days, weeks and months, but he is concerned with things such as fullness and opportunity. Try and think more 'egg-timer' than 'alarm clock'. Think as if every day is the day, but don't go to bed disappointed if it's not – maybe it will be tomorrow. Whenever it is, it will be at just the right time.

Dancing in the Moonlight

Ever since I married Grace, I've been living in a flat slap bang in the city centre of Manchester. If anything's going on, we know about it; we just need to open the window! Some nights are bonkers, absolute chaos! Since they've shut down Wembley Stadium, a lot of the international footy matches have come to Old Trafford. Of course all the fans want to go on a bit of a bender after the match and we get all the gruesome aerial shots.

While all this was going on outside one night, I was safely removed from the action, watching the highlights on TV. In the post-match interview, Garth Crookes interviewed David Beckham, Teddy Sheringham and Sven-Göran Eriksson. Every one of them talked about one thing. Character.

What is 'character'?

If you're into football or Robbie Williams, you'll know the song 'You only sing when you're winning!' Fans holler it across a stadium, effectively accusing the other fans of having no character. Character is something special that lives deep in the human soul and keeps you going forward in life. It keeps you singing, even when you're losing.

We're convinced that God is real and we read his book – the Bible. It's full of people full of character. Think about that bloke called Paul. Among writing half of the New Testament, he wrote the letter to the Romans. It says there in chapter 5 'Character produces Hope.' People full of character are people full of hope! England didn't play so hard that night just to keep fit! Those nutters on the terraces at Old Trafford weren't singing so loudly because they all thought they were on *Stars in their Eyes*! They had hope! They were all hoping to go on and win the World Cup. Anybody else hoping for that? I've been hoping for it all my life!

The team also showed their character in their demonstration of how to persevere. The two are totally linked together. Go back to Romans 5 and have a look. I watched David Beckham take half-a-dozen free kicks during the game and none went in. Then, in the ninety-second minute, the lineman's flag went up... There was nothing I could do about it. There was nothing any of the 67,000 people in that stadium could do about it. We were completely powerless to win that game. It was a horrible feeling. Nobody watching the game was good enough to take a shot like that at a moment like that. But at just the right time, Beckham, who just would not give up, sent it through the defending wall and stuck it in the top left corner! Get in!

There will be times, not a few but many times, when you will have the opportunity to jack it in. Nobody is immune from it. Listen to Billy Graham.

'I had nothing to give. I had exhausted my material. I had exhausted my body. I had exhausted my mind. Yet the preaching had far more power. It was God taking sheer weakness – it is when I get out of the way and say, "God, You have to do it."

I sat on that platform many nights with nothing to say, nothing. And I knew that in a few minutes, I'd have to get up and preach, and I'd just say, "Oh, God, I can't do it!"

And yet, I would stand up and all of a sudden, it would begin to come... just God giving it, that's all.'

Depending on God is where it's at. Billy got that sorted right back in the early days. Talk about character! The guy is a legend. Massive success with dollops of grace. A welcome contrast to many involved in evangelism over the years who've lived and preached a warped picture of God, thinking they're doing him a favour. They've scared the hell out of people and burnt themselves out in the process. They've preached one message from a platform and practised another one in the back room. It is cost, yes, but it is also eternal gain. It is sowing in tears but it is reaping in joy. It is charisma but it's about character. Character is what you are in secret. It's about embodying the hope in Jesus Christ who died for all while the world was still living life with two fingers held up to him.

Fruit of the Spirit

I've heard it said that the Holy Ghost makes flesh nervous. Think about it. This is God, after all, not just some random Jedi electric force field. The Holy Spirit is as much a person as the Father or the Son. He has will, emotion and creativity. One thing that the Holy Spirit makes a lot of is fruit. And I'm not talking about bananas.

I don't claim to be an expert on fruit. As a bachelor, I would go to the supermarket and at the bottom of my trolley of pizzas and sad meals for one would be a lonely apple, comforted only by a tangerine. For a while, I tried to grow some fruit in the office. I had a spider plant on my window ledge which I used to sing Louis Armstrong to – it never responded, though, not so much as a raisin out of it! Hopefully your serving God will prove to be more fruitful than that.

'...the fruit of the Spirit is love, joy, peace, patience, kindness, goodness, faithfulness, gentleness, and self-control' (Gal 5:22,23).

I want to take a bit of a detour from the 'fruit' of 'souls in the kingdom' to look at the fruit of our personal relationships with our Lord. Lets have a look at this, fruit amateurs that we are!

Check your Crop

Jesus said that '...by their fruit, you will know them...' and that '...a bad tree cannot bear good fruit...'. Clearly, living as a community of Christians, it will be obvious to those around us whether or not we're happening with God. We may not show it in the way we pray, the way we sing or the way we raise our hands but the signs will begin to show, as we display a lack or abundance of these nine key ingredients. I've devised a little light-hearted exercise to diagnose how we're doing in different parts of our spiritual life. The New Year is a great time to do this – you can set goals, implement changes and look back to make sure you're improving in your weak areas! Check out the Fruitometer over the page.

No Root – No Fruit!

Unless you're a fruit bowl. Have you all realised this yet? It's amazing how many people genuinely love Jesus but miss out on all he's got for them by wandering off, just as things are getting interesting. Think about the parable of the sower – one of the most famous stories Jesus told (Matt 13). He painted a picture of different kinds of people and how they respond to the word. The clear conclusion was that if you don't have roots, you're going to fade away in the heat of the sun. But if your roots go deep, you'll produce a bumper crop. Again, Jesus stresses the point, this time with the illustration of a vine; eleven times in the first ten verses of John chapter 15, he uses the word 'remain', and he mentions fruit seven times. What's his point? Well, if you haven't got it yet, you can't be a fruitful tumbleweed! To be an effective servant of Jesus, you must be part of the big picture.

I call this checklist the FRUITOMETER.

The Fruitometer

HUMBUG ———————————————————— HONEY
love

RAIN ———————————————————— SHINE
joy

HURRICANE ———————————————————— ZEPHYR
peace

WASP ———————————————————— SNAIL
patience

SALT ———————————————————— SUGAR
kindness

EMINEM ———————————————————— BRITNEY!!!
goodness

PETER STRINGFELLOW ———————————————————— CLIFF RICHARD
faithfulness

GODZILLA ———————————————————— LASSIE
gentleness

PANTS ———————————————————— OVERCOAT
self-control

Fly or Dung?

Here's a bit of a brain-teaser. You have to co-operate here; it's where the book gets interactive.

'Fly or dung. Which is best?'

If you think dung is best, hold your nose and go 'Pheeew!'

If you think fly is best, squat on your chair and go 'Zzzzzzzzzzzt!'

What's all that about? Well, flies buzz in and out of your tree, sucking on your fruit and leaving scabs all over it. Then they just buzz off again and do the same to someone else's tree. Dung, on the other hand, will stick with you, ooze out and fertilise; dung is there for the long term and won't buzz off. So clearly, it's better to be dung than fly. You must have gathered by now how much I like to drop in a bit of the Old King James when I'm making a point. Well, check this. *'Why cumbereth it the ground? ...I shall dig it and dung it...'* ! (Luke 13:6–9)

Make it your business to be dung, not fly. Flies are greedy and will eat anything, even dung! Flies are only in relationships for what they can get. Dung always gives. Who's ever heard someone teach on dung before? You get it here first every time.

No Scrumping!

Do you know what 'scrumping' is? Hands up!

'Scrumping' is pinching someone's fruit. And that works for fruit of the Spirit, too. Perhaps not deliberately, but by manipulating love, absorbing joy or disrupting peace, you can leave your friends bare. If you live like this, not only will you ruin everyone else's crop, you'll never actually grow your own. Let me give you a personal example:

I'd been going out with Grace for about six months. We were in the LDR stage. Long distance relationship. One of the problems with this was that when we did get together, if we weren't careful, things could get pretty steamy. We're married now and she's happy for me to tell you this, as it might help you. After stepping over the line too many times and getting slapped, I got down in prayer to examine my heart. God spoke to me about self-control and how to grow some. Every time I began to get frisky, Grace would call the shots but this meant that I was scrumping – stealing her fruit. I was depending on her self-control because mine was useless. We talked and prayed together and God did turn things around. In a typically God way, he turned what could have been a tricky situation to grow me in a new way. Now I try to call my own shots in all kinds of ways.

365 Days a Year

This might sound strange, but producing fruit takes work. Do you know that if you were to photocopy 365 of those fruitometers and pray every morning to improve your harvest and every night evaluate how you'd done, I guarantee that it would be the most fruitful year of your life. But it's too much like hard work. Are we prepared to put in the graft? This certainly isn't a conventional fruit tree. What sort of picture do you have in mind? This whole plant thing makes you think that growing fruit is a passive job but remember, it's just an illustration – it's not real! We don't walk around with a great big patience dangling around our hips and a tiny withered joy tucked shyly behind our ear. These are vital qualities of character which take working at. Peter, talking on the same subject, put it differently:

'…make every effort to add to your faith goodness; and to goodness, knowledge; and to knowledge, self-control; and to self-control, perseverance; and to perseverance, godliness; and to godliness, brotherly kindness; and to brotherly kindness, love. For if you possess these qualities in increasing measure they will keep you from being ineffective and unproductive in your knowledge of our Lord Jesus Christ.' (2 Pet 1:5–8)

God of all Comfort

So we've recognised that in the purposes of God we must wait for his perfect timing. We've seen that character is the all-important quality to see us through. We know that on the way, we will bear all kinds of fruit in our lives. But there's one more thought I'd like to leave with you. Your Father has a vested interest in keeping you going through all the rough stuff that life throws at you. It's God's job to sustain you as you stand in the gap for this generation. When it gets tough, remember that you are not the first saint ever to suffer for the gospel! Your head may be telling you to pack up and go back to your mum's house where the bed is always made and the tea is always in the pot. At these times, cling to God and hold everything else lightly. In the opening of his deeply personal second letter to the Corinthians, Paul describes how he found himself in this place.

God has a million ways to surprise and sustain you, usually not the ways that you've been thinking of but he will 'keep' you.

'Praise be to the God and Father of our Lord Jesus Christ, the Father of compassion and the God of all comfort, who comforts us in all our troubles, so that we can comfort those in any trouble with the comfort we ourselves have received from God. For just as the sufferings of Christ flow over into our lives, so also through Christ our comfort overflows. If we are distressed, it is for your comfort and salvation; if we are comforted, it is for your comfort, which produces in you patient endurance of the same sufferings we suffer. And our hope for you is firm, because we know that just as you share in our sufferings, so also you share in our comfort. We do not want you to be uninformed, brothers, about the hardships we suffered in the province of Asia. We were under great pressure, far beyond our ability to endure, so that we despaired even of life. Indeed, in our hearts we felt the sentence of death. But this happened that we might not rely on ourselves but on God, who raises the dead. He has delivered us from such a deadly peril, and he will deliver us. On him we have set our hope that he will continue to deliver us, as you help us by your prayers. Then many will give thanks on our behalf for the gracious favour granted us in answer to the prayers of many.'

God has a million ways to surprise and sustain you, usually not the ways that you've been thinking of but he will 'keep' you. That's a little-understood biblical idea which carries over from the Old Testament. It springs from a Hebrew word which means 'prickly hedge', the kind of barrier used by the owners of vineyards and orchards to protect their precious fruit-bearing trees from wild animals and thieves. It forms part of a blessing that God gave to Moses to declare over Israel, the children of promise.

'The LORD bless you and keep you;
the LORD make his face shine upon you and be gracious to you;
the LORD turn his face towards you and give you peace.' (Num 6:24–26)

It's a blessing which now overflows to us, inheritors of the promise by faith. God constantly proves incredibly creative and resourceful in his determination to keep on blessing us as we graft away here in Manchester. Take, for instance, this letter, which arrived out of the blue, written to one of our team leaders who was really needing some encouragement.

'Dear 'Salford lovers', smile,
I read on the website that you are tired and waiting for new people to come and work with you. I read it and was touched. I know so well how you feel! And I wanna share with you by sharing, encourage you. Through what you have started in Manchester (Eden projects,) I started doing the same in Holland. When I was 21, I moved back to the area of south Holland where I grew up and I started living in a poor area of town. Alone. My house became an open house soon and kids and teens came in. After living there three years, the house became too small for all the kids so I moved. That was in September 2001. We (me and my husband – since 2 months) have seen how God works in mighty ways these last months! We have 240 kids coming to us now, 1,000 regularly (once a week). We have six workers with us, all spending some hours a week with us. And they caught the vision and wanna go for it (though they have limited time now). God is moving... and it's great, but not easy: 70% of the kids coming are Muslim. The area is socially very poor (financially, too). We feel alone so often. But God is rich and he keeps us going. Yes, I know how it feels to be tired of it all. Loving it, working for it, but being tired as well. And I wanna encourage you. Keep looking for all the little lights around you. Keep finding little changes in the kids around. And keep trusting God. He will never give you more than you can handle. Stay close to him! And keep on going: you help people like my husband and me to keep going as well. Thank you very much! We pray for you and love you – though we have never met!'

Isn't that absolutely awesome? It was sent by a couple from Holland. God is massive! He cares enough to move someone's heart in a completely different country to meet the emotional need he perceives in another one of his precious children. Don't ever think that God isn't interested or that he's too busy for you. He senses your every heartbeat. He feels your every breath. If you are really having a hard time at the moment, don't give in to discouragement or cynicism. Hang in there, you aren't alone; God is with you. He makes it clear in his Word that he will cause you to grow through these trials and he won't test you beyond what you can bear. Peter lets us know this in the first of his letters:

'Be self-controlled and alert. Your enemy the devil prowls around like a roaring lion looking for someone to devour. Resist him, standing firm in the faith, because you know that your brothers throughout the world are undergoing the same kind of sufferings.

And the God of all grace, who called you to his eternal glory in Christ, after you have suffered a little while, will himself restore you and make you strong, firm and steadfast.'

If you're struggling a bit even as you read this book, you might want to pause for a little while, get out your Bible and read Psalm 63. Read it three or four times until it really sinks in.

If you're on cloud nine and being blessed out of your socks every time you step out of the door, then you might want to pause as well and spend some time interceding for those who aren't knowing many high points at the moment.

section 4

xcelerate!

During the early stages of an *Xcelerate* course, we make a deliberate effort to challenge our raw recruits about what they think they are capable of. One method of evangelism that scares the pants off everyone is Streetwork – aaaaaaaaggghhh! Most of that mortal fear is simply a fear of the unknown. Taking a considerate relational approach out to the street can be really rewarding and great fun. The prayer times before going out are full of those wonderful desperate 'God, I really need you now!' prayers. Rarely do the guys and girls come back anything but buzzing.

On a recent 'Power Hour', I paired up with a young fella called Jonathan. The 'hook' on this particular excursion was 'Excuse me, have you seen today's *Daily Mirror*?'. The group had chosen various stories which they thought would make engaging talking points for passers-by. One story was a particularly gruesome tale of 'bystander apathy' when a teenage girl had been gang-raped in broad daylight. Many people had hurriedly passed by, careful not to get involved. A real modern day 'Good Samaritan' parable, except that the Good Samaritan never showed up. The piece ended with a powerful quote from the girl's mother questioning the kind of society that we've become.

After a number of abbreviated exchanges in the Gay Village area of Manchester, we kept moving towards Chinatown. We spotted a young man who looked as though he might have a bit of time on his hands and Jonathan asked him if he had a minute to spare. In no time at all, we'd established that he certainly would have 'kicked off' and done all that he could to help the girl. So we prodded him a bit further, trying to get to the root of his motivations; why did he have such a well developed sense of right and wrong when the rest of the world was becoming numb? Forty-five minutes later, we were still going! We covered everything, Jesus, the church, the whole gospel, forwards, backwards and forwards again. Neither of us could have imagined it going so well, short of his falling on his knees there and then. From his initial hostility to our suggestion that God might be for real, he opened right up, to the extent that he said that next time he was in a jam, he'd be praying.

Now, clearly, that's not quite the kind of 'weeping in the streets' drama you usually find in books on evangelism but we think it was a result. You know the best bit; you can do it today. Those boundaries you think you have – they don't exist. Let go and allow yourself to be *Xcelerated*!

sounds of
the city

The city is not a concrete jungle,
it is a human zoo.
Desmond Morris

Strange Affection

My great affection for the cities of the world has steadily grown to become one of the most dominant motivators in my life. It doesn't really add up. I was brought up on a council estate on the edge of heaven, post-war potting sheds on the edge of the Peak District. 'Derbyshire born, Derbyshire bred, Derbyshire wed and Derbyshire dead' was the local expectation. I went on friendsreunited.com the other night only to find that most of my old pals from school were still living in the same street.

What happened to me? I used really to like the countryside... well I still do – but the trees I used to climb and the lakes I used to swim in don't have the 'wow' factor any more. Instead, I find myself drooling at the concrete curves of the Mancunian Way.

My wife is an architect, and we chat about the future of our city all the time. That's a bit of a fib actually, she talks about great cities like London, New York and Paris and I bash on monotonously about my beloved Manchester. One of the world's foremost city-shapers is a chap called Sir Richard Rogers. Grace's claim to fame, and claim to shame, is that she turned down a job with him to marry me. Sorry Richie! In his 1997 book, *Cities for a small planet* , he shows just how critical the health of the city is for the health of the world:

'Cities have never contained so many nor so large a proportion of the human race. Between 1950 and 1990, the population of the world's cities increased ten-fold, soaring from 200 million to more than 2 billion. The future of civilisation will be determined by its cities and in its cities.'

Romans 8 describes that as:

'The creation waits in eager expectation for the sons of God to be revealed. For the creation was subjected to frustration, not by its own choice, but by the will of the one who subjected it, in hope that the creation itself will be liberated from its bondage to decay and brought into the glorious freedom of the children of God.'

You don't get images of fluffy bunnies skipping in the meadow with la-la lambs, do you? If the kingdom is to come at all, it must come to our cities.

Street Level

Ever taken time to read the street? Fly posters, leaflets on the pavement. Graffiti – the cool stuff and the scribble; read the walls – there's a noise. It's in phone boxes, passing snippets of conversations, across the road in an argument, the interruptions of beggars and scam artists. There's indigestion in the belly of the city, too many late nights and early mornings. Are you there for your city? Yes, *your* city. So you live in a town or a village? Well, where's your city? All the stats show that, in the UK, the massive majority of Christians live out in the leafy suburbs or the rolling rural expanses. I want to challenge you to take an interest in your city. Yes, the big scary smelly place that you get in and out of as quickly as you can.

It's no wonder that sensible people want to stay away from cities; after all, in the UK, 75% of crime takes place in five cities. One of them is Manchester – but I wouldn't be anywhere else in the world. Our cities need God in a massive way. These dark places desperately need the light of Jesus but the light is under a bushel, a nice rhododendron, surrounded by a neatly trimmed privet to be precise. A twentieth-century writer by the name of Cyril Connolly penned these incisive words.

'Slums may well be the breeding grounds of crime, but middle class suburbs are the incubators of apathy and delirium.'

Let me throw some more statistics at you. How about this? The Bible mentions cities 816 times. Just to put that in context, it mentions love 690 times. If you also counted all the mentions of specific cities, you'd be there all day; you can hardly turn a page without a city forming part of the scene. The Bible shows us that the eternal purpose of God begins in a garden and climaxes in a city. It teaches us of the epic tale of two cities, the glory of Zion and the corruption of Babylon. As we near the end of this book, I want to take a few risks. I want to risk telling you that if you don't like hanging out in cities, you are going to have a rough time in eternity. Heaven isn't quite the serene wheatfield which Maximus dreams of in the blockbuster movie *Gladiator*. In many ways, it's far more like the Rome he was so keen to leave. Take a trip to your city sometime soon. Slow down, breathe deeply and open your eyes.

Bus Stop Perspective

There was a time when I think that my custom alone was keeping the fleet of smelly old Manchester buses on the road. I practically lived on the flea-bitten things. If you were to join together all the journeys I went on during the period '92 to '96, back to back, you'd be travelling for over eight weeks. And how many memorable conversations did I have with my fellow passengers? You've got it, zero. Yes, you've got to the end of the book only to discover that I am in fact the world's worst evangelist. Trust me. I've argued with God:

'Why didn't you make me like those wonderful weird people who can chat to a total stranger like an old friend? Why was I brought up British?'

You've met these infuriating people, haven't you? (Apologies if you are one!) These people have no fear of parking their buttocks down on that empty seat right next to someone, even though there is a double empty seat just behind. That's not in the rules! You fill up the double empties first, then, and only then, do you sit next to someone. And you must not talk. Look straight ahead. Breathe quietly. Do not smile. These flagrant cultural rule-breakers just start gossiping away. How do they do it? I really do want to know. Sell me your gifting!

Now if someone makes the first move, I'm fine. I'll chat all day. Of course, like a good Christian I'll often try to coax my fellow passengers into conversations. Don't tell me you've never done it. The train is best for this, longer journeys and the boredom factor means people tend to be that little bit more open to chat. You open your bag, and heave out a deliberately huge Christian tome with a gold embossed title, something like *God's Lovetastic Plan for the Universe*. You thumb it craftily, watching the eyes of the seat-dwellers opposite. Which one of them will fall under its power first? How long will it take before their rampant curiosity causes them to question you about its origins? But does it get you into a conversation? Oh, the British reserve. How do we break through it?

We've been really blessed to have two or three 'proper' evangelists on each *Xcelerate* course so far. They arrive in the morning with awesome stories of people who God has caused them to collide with. They've been explaining the gospel and praying with people. Half of me is jumping up and down with excitement and the other half is thinking:

'God, why am I running this programme? I'm just not cut out for this evangelism lark; that never happens to me.'

There's only one thing to do at time like that. Tie up my shoelaces, clear some space in my diary and take my body out into the vacuum, the places where I can find people who need Jesus. Places like bus stops, which, incidentally, is where I'm writing this chapter right now. It's dark, it's flipping cold, it's Saturday night. The traffic's getting heavier and bodies seem to be materialising right out of the exhaust fumes and brake lights, handbags and gladrags shining almost neon. A pack of young scallies bowls past, splitting cans as they go, almost as young as the night. Determine in your heart to go. Widen your sphere. The tribes need you.

I went through a difficult patch a year or two ago. At the time, I got pretty shaky. I was working for God really hard and fairly directly, too. My mind was doing loops on me, though, and my body felt ready to fall to bits as well. To compound things I knew that I was spending too much time in the Christian ghetto, trapped there. I'd programmed a welcome note into my mobile phone, COME ON SOLDIER. It greeted me every morning for at least a month, giving me the sliver of hope that I needed to face the day. All in all, not a good place to be.

One morning in church, God caused a snapshot sequence to appear in my mind. It was a chessboard, and the game had reached a critical stage. I saw that God valued me as part of his strategy but that I was under threat and he didn't want to lose me. He showed me that I wasn't the only useful piece in this game and I saw his hand move me back to a less vulnerable position. The image really stuck with me. Remarkably, within a very short space of time, I found myself experiencing what I can only explain as God's extravagant kindness. With minimum hassle, I was relocated to a place away from unnecessary danger until the time was right to shift me back up to the front line,. Which, I can say, he totally has. Now my phone welcomes me with a very different message, NOW IS THE TIME. I'm back in the places where the people are, even though I'm still useless at those opening lines, so here goes.

'What bus you waiting for, mate?'

Solution for Society

For some time, we've been enjoying the benefits of a partnership with the Shaftesbury Society. They're a huge Christian action organisation whose founder, Lord Shaftesbury, was an inspirational mover and shaker in the social and Labour reform movement of the nineteenth century. He was particularly moved by the plight of children in the fast-growing cities of the time, many of whom were working sixteen-hour shifts in factories from the age of six! In fact, his first success was to make it illegal for any child under nine to be employed by mill owners, and for under thirteens to work a maximum ten-hour day. This was not even 150 years ago. Now his legacy is carried on throughout the UK through the work of guys like Chris Erskine whose development work on *EDEN* and the *LifeCentre*, and we've been blessed with some really valuable insights into how God wants to make himself known to the world. At a recent leaders' lunch attended by ministers from around Manchester I heard Chris say, in the spirit of Ephesians 3:10:

'The church needs to stop coming up with social strategies and realise that it is a social strategy.'

How deep is that? When you consider what the church has historically become known as and compare it to a statement like that, you start to realise the degree of change which has to occur during our generation just to bring us within sight of God's original intention for his body on the earth. Are you going to allow the church to continue being shaped by society in the twenty-first century or are you going to be a reformer, causing the church to affect society once again? Prolific American author and academic Martin Oppenheimer describes the challenge we face in stark terms.

'Today's city is the most vulnerable social structure ever conceived by man.'

It's my firm belief that if we can get it right in our cities, we can get it right anywhere. It's been a long time since anyone recognised it but evangelists play a massive part in this. Not loose cannon evangelists, causing chaos on the deck, but evangelists enabled through team to bring in the raw 'people material' that makes up our community of love, life, grace, acceptance and forgiveness. The church in this sense, to the new believer, is the joy of meeting long-lost family, the connection with divine destiny. As someone far more eloquent than me said, *'In the absence of a great dream, pettiness prevails.'*

Ooooh, I'm getting all carried away now. Forgive me; this stuff floats my boat! And while I'm fired up, let me urge you one more time to venture out of your comfort zones. Get out there and test the boundaries of your abilities. Actively resist the urge to brake and take seriously the challenge to accelerate.

voice of a
generation

It is our choices, Harry,
that show what we truly are,
far more than our abilities.
Albus Dumbledore

One Voice

This is the last chapter and I've been thrilled to have the opportunity to speak to the most powerful group of people in the world. That's you, by the way! Do you know where you fit into history? Especially those of you born after 1980, you Millennials? You are the global generation; you have a common language. You have more in common with your generation across the world than with your own parents. That's why *Eminem* can sell so many records like:

'...a billion of em who cuss like me, look like me, just don't give a **** like me.'

A year or so ago, I was with a bunch of teenagers in a refugee-populated slum area of Azerbaijan. They grinned and came out with phrases they expected me to connect with:

'Jack Daniels, Jean Claude van Damme, David Beckham...'

Around that time, there was also a story all over the news of some UN soldiers taken hostage in Somalia by one of the most dangerous militia groups known in that volatile corner of Africa, who go by the name 'The West Side Boys'. What the BBC was ashamed to tell us is that they are essentially just teenagers, driven by the voice of their prophet, Tupac Shakur. The generation is rising and it's recognised. Naomi Klein, in her multi-million selling *No Logo*, tells the story of a youth worker in the Bronx who, together with his group, took on one of the biggest corporate powers on the planet, *Nike*. For as long as they could remember, the company had consistently ripped off them and their mates. They weren't impressed and decided that they didn't want their *Nike* products any more, so they were going to give them back. They had their moment outside *Nike Town* on Fifth Avenue in New York. TV cameras from every network across the US were there; it was the biggest PR disaster in the whole of *Nike*'s history. A thirteen-year-old activist from the Bronx delivered this message to the nation.

'Nike, we made you. We can break you.'

You know your cause; now let your voice be heard. I've written this book because I believe in you. I'm a GEN X; we were born in the sixties and the seventies. They've labelled us 'the generation terrorists', 'the jilted generation'. We're fighting our own battle. I want to get you ready for yours. Conditions have never been better for an explosion of God across the globe. I expect to see it with my own eyes. Are you ready to reveal Jesus through the things you say and the way you live? That's what it will take.

Generational Connections

There is no better place to find out about the connection of generations than in the Bible. No matter who is studying, Christian or not, no other book has the unique content of the Bible. It outlines a sequence of promises and discoveries handed down from one generation to the next from the dawn of time until the present day and beyond. Families, tribes, nations and kingdoms rise and fall. The Bible shows the way that one person with a clear revelation can shape the destiny of decade upon decade. There is the sense of continuity as new characters emerge, each one 'standing on the shoulders of giants'.

In the Bible, we see God's purpose carried out through successive revelations to successive generations. Take the boy Samuel, for instance; let's get a picture of how God worked in and through him. Sam always looked a bit of a state. Eli should've known that he was destined to be a prophet; he was probably nicknamed 'Crusty' or something like that. In 1 Samuel 1:11, Sam's mum makes a crazy vow to God that the boy's hair will never be cut. Have you ever wondered what kind of mad stuff your mum prayed before you were born? Eeek! So by the age of about eight, Sam would've had pretty advanced dreadlocks, but then, of course, there's his 'little robe' (1 Sam 2:19). The poor lad would get a new T-shirt once a year – yuk! As if that weren't too much for the poor urchin to bear, he was made to live in a tent (1 Sam 3:3). Your New International Version may well have tricked you into thinking that Samuel slept in the temple, but of course, the temple wasn't going to be built for almost a hundred years. Sam slept in the tabernacle and there is no indication of any moaning about that. In fact, you get the impression that Sam was a real blessing, serving the old priest. The only sad thing in the story is that he didn't expect to hear God for himself! Fortunately, God had determined to change that and, according to his established pattern, opened up his purpose in the generation through a revelation, a word, an encounter.

Revelation is emerging in your generation. You're at a defining stage. You are coming of age. 1 Samuel 3:11 is great; pay attention to the language, the grace and the heart. Remember that the Lord is speaking to a boy who's never heard his voice before.

'And the Lord said to Samuel: "See, I am about to do something in Israel that *will make the ears of everyone who hears of it tingle." '*

My ears are tingling already. I can't tell you what your revelation is, because then it would be mine, not yours! You must have your own insight. All I can tell you is that in previous generations, God's radical revelation has simply been a rediscovery of his original and eternal intention. You won't be able to keep it to yourself. Suddenly, you'll find a dramatically fresh use for your vocal cords. Jeremiah, who also started hearing from God at an early age, knew this all too well. In his later years, he put the sensation into words.

'His word is in my heart like a fire, a fire shut up in my bones. I am weary of holding it in; indeed I cannot' (Jer 20:9).

I am one hundred per cent confident that if your heart longs to beat in time with God's, if you spend time calling out to him, he will most definitely speak to you. Learn these three lessons from the giants of history.

1. Be available. That is, the 'Here I am…' a phrase on the lips of Samuel, and also of Abraham, Jacob, Moses, Isaiah and Jesus Christ himself. It's not a statement of geography. God knows where you are. It's a statement of availability. God needs to know that you're ready.

2. Be listening. Our boy Sam, with a bit of help from the old fella, got that locked down in chapter 3 verse 10. From that moment on, he took the initiative in developing an awesome listening ear. There was no way he was returning to the dire straits described in chapter 3 verse 1.

   'The word of the Lord was rare; there were not many visions.'

3. Be responsive. In chapter 3 verse 17, even Samuel was tempted to keep the word of God to himself. That would have been a seriously bad habit to get into. Fortunately, Eli prised it out of him under threat of a bit of divine retribution! In your own life, take immediate steps to work out even the slightest, simplest word. Your generation needs to hear your voice.

The Final Word

I do feel that I've said plenty, for now, anyway. I hope that this book has helped to equip you and examine your life in the echo of God's heartbeat. To all the *Xcelerators* past, present and future, 'Rispek!' It's your time to come on through.

Emily, 23
now working as an inner city youth worker

I believe sincerely that winning people for Jesus is all about integrity. It's about living and breathing in the Holy Spirit; about everything that you do. You can't simply expect people to believe you or listen to you if you say you're a Christian but ignore it and go your own way in your actions. People won't respect you for that. These young people are looking for truth – something that 'works'. In this way, you can't compartmentalise God; he's living and active in every part of our lives. That means that when we're out there on the streets, so is God. We sometimes forget that we're the closest some of these young people will ever get to knowing Jesus, and it's vital that we live that way. God's heart beats fast for every one of the kids we've worked with and it's so important to remember this. Something that God has taught me continually this year is that we need time and patience. Building meaningful relationships with young people takes a lot of time and energy, but each of them is so well worth it to God. You can't simply expect to come into their lives and be accepted straight away because many young people have been let down in the past and need to know whom to trust. God's heart is for hurting people to be healed and to come to a relationship with him, so the evangelist's heartbeat must beat sensitively with a genuine love for people which draws them to Jesus. It's so important for us to reach out to people with this love, which should be evident throughout the whole of our lives.

Dan, 19
now at Uni in Lancaster

I finished the course and a few months later, went on to University. This was the testing time for me, as all throughout the course, I had felt a particular calling towards the curious tribe known as 'students'. Now I had to back it up with some action. I finally had to put my money where my mouth was – not that I have any money as a student – and try to make an impact on a culture of which I was now very much a part. It is a lot easier to claim to be called to witness to a group when you aren't there among them; once you are there, it's a much harder thing to do.

It took me a while to find my feet. I cannot claim to have ushered in revival since I arrived here but nor have I sat idle. For me, the evangelist's heartbeat starts racing when there are fresh challenges afoot, when I am forced to share the gospel and when I'm flippin' scared. Nobody ever said that evangelism was easy and I doubt many people find it so, but it is something to which we are all called and it is an honour to call myself an evangelist. I have the privilege to share the truth that Jesus Christ died for my sins so that I might be forgiven and be forever accepted by God.

When you put it like that, beans on toast for the umpteenth time doesn't sound quite so bad.

Laura, 19
about to start a music and media degree

On *Xcelerate*, one of the main methods of transport we depended on was the bus system. One Thursday, after finishing an afternoon placement, I was on my way home, waiting for a bus in the city centre. For the previous week or so, God had been on my case about telling people about him on buses, as I was spending so much time on them!

On this occasion, I got on the bus and the Holy Spirit blatantly prompted me to speak to the lady next to me. But, my human instinct kicked in and I began to concoct every excuse I could not to speak to her, as I felt very self-conscious in this quiet bus! My heart was beating fast, but eventually I said to her,

'Er, excuse me, you may think this is a bit strange, but I feel I need to tell you that God loves you, and that you're really important to him…'

At this, she looked at me, puzzled, and said,

'I'm sorry, you'll have to speak more clearly. I'm from the Czech Republic.'

Great! The one person God wanted me to speak to didn't even speak much English! But I said the whole lot again, slower and louder(!), so the whole bus ended up getting blasted with the gospel, too! In the end, I missed my stop and found myself over half an hour away from home. Realising her English was okay, the conversation progressed from my explaining the gospel to her asking endless questions of how I became a Christian, what it meant to me, and where she could start going to church. I was buzzin'!

When we obey God and step beyond comfort zones, no matter how inadequate or stupid we feel, he can and will raise the spiritual temperature in people's lives, so that they move that bit closer to heaven.

chapter
thirteen

Vron, 27
now running a youth project in the South East

I have spent time recently getting much closer to God and it feels as if I'm seeing through 'new eyes'! I have an expectation in my heart that is nearly bursting out and know that God is gonna do some big stuff here. I hope to see a real change in the young people I work with and feel God stirring them up. We have done a Get God course which has been great; seventeen came each week! Now we're talking about doing a weekly 'Youth Church' type thing because there are a few teenagers who are totally fired up but don't have anywhere to go for it. Have to admit, I'm not convinced that a separate church is a good thing but when faced with those kinds of needs, drastic action is needed! Need to pray a lot more first, though!

While doing *Xcelerate*, I got a glimpse of how God feels about his lost children. For those who have nothing and those who think they have it all, he weeps with a broken heart. When someone can see the Spirit of God in us, something amazing happens; his or her life will change, sometimes slowly. Problems may not disappear but life will come! When I get closer and closer to God, I see things happen; young people, especially, hungering to know or to be with God. The most exciting thing is that, although I'm seeing these things now, I still have such a way to go. What more does God have waiting for us? You see, I can do any good deed, help many people in my own strength, but without God working through me, any solutions will always be short-lived. Believe me, I've tried!

'He who abides in me, and I in him, bears much fruit: for without me you can do nothing, (John 15:5). People need to see Jesus, not me.

Rachel, 22
now chasing God in the Midlands

One night while on *Xcelerate*, my housemate and I had an awesome time of prayer in which God spoke so clearly to us both, not just to pray for opportunities to share the gospel but to get out there and do it and he meant then, that night! Even more of a 'God moment' was when, during this prayer time, God put the exact same place in Manchester on both our hearts. We both knew God had someone he wanted us to evangelise to that very night so without delay, we trekked off into Manchester. As we arrived where God had told us to go, we sat on some steps, praying God would show us specifically who to talk to. Sitting there on those steps, watching the people go on by, God was showing us what it was like to be homeless. God then gave us both the same picture of a guy and within seconds, we saw him across the street. Wow! What a God moment! We went to chat to the guy and ended up there for hours, telling him about God's awesome love for him. He wept as we spoke, saying he'd never heard any of this before, then we had the amazing privilege of praying for him. God's tears just wept from us, too, as God showed us what it was to have an evangelist's heartbeat. No one had given this guy the time of day for years. I know one hundred per cent that God put me in that guy's life for that time to share the amazing truth of what Jesus has done for me and could do for this amazing guy as well. Praise God for these opportunities! Let's never turn them down but grab every one we get!

Kieran, 18
now at uni in Glasgow

To win this generation for Jesus, you need to have the heart of Jesus. You need to have love and passion. Today people see through you if you're not real, genuine and passionate. If you don't believe what you're saying, neither will they. Love is the key; if you show people love and meet people where they are, they will listen to you and you can start to influence them and see their life change. Love is all – consuming, and the love that you need is love for them, love for their situation, but most of all love for God. With a strong relationship with God yourself, God will give you some of his heart, and a compassion for the lost. The evangelist's heartbeat needs to catch the heartbeat of God. Combine that love with a passion, a passion that makes you desperate to see people's lives change, to improve things for them, and people will respect you. Don't treat people like statistics. Be friends with your natural friends, enjoying their friendship and don't just see them as a project. People are worth so much more than mere projects. Most of all, let people watch your life. If you're living for God, that will shine through and that is the single biggest thing that we can do for him and them.

Jenny, 19
now working for The Message

Catching the heartbeat of God was really not something I did a lot of before coming on *Xcelerate*. Right from the start, we were encouraged to be aware of 'God prods'. It often blew my mind how much God really answered my prayers. Quite a lot of the time, he took me way out of my depth and I had to rely on him completely. On a Wednesday, Kieran and I were working with The Mustard Tree, an organisation which works with the homeless. They asked us to go out onto the streets and talk to the homeless people. It was something I had never done before, so we decided to pray that God would show us who to speak to. We wandered around until we met a guy named Tom, who was quite 'out of it' on drugs but we decided to stop and talk to him. He told us all about his alcohol and drug problems, and we told him we were Christians. As we left, he asked if he could have a hug, something he hadn't had for a long time; we told him we would come again next week. We continued to visit him for the rest of the five months, and we really felt that we were taking Jesus onto the streets. Week by week, Tom improved. Even today, when I go into town, he remembers me and asks if I am still friends with God. It really taught me how God can use you, more than you can imagine.

Mark, 20
now working for a church in Leeds

Without faith, the evangelist is nothing; faith is the true evangelist's heartbeat. We need faith in what we preach; we need faith to believe that Jesus was who he said he was. We need to be able to trust that God will reward our sowing and we will reap a harvest. We need faith to get out of our comfortable lifestyles and associate ourselves with the sort of people Jesus hung out with.

We can trust that the word of God is true and is all we need. By faith, we can be sure that the Spirit of God is on us because he has anointed us to preach the good news. And you can be sure that your life and ministry will bind up the broken-hearted and give freedom to those bound by the chains of oppression, guilt, sorrow and sin!

So go for it. Be like Paul; develop a relationship with God that's so intimate you can trust everything he says, live it and pass it on. Live by such a strong faith that it's infectious! And when this generation sees in God's people someone they can trust completely, they'll come flocking to Jesus!!

David, 21
now working for Signpost International

After an intense month's training, the Going Global team has experienced its first week in the Philippines. God has been amazing and from the start, the team has seen God use it so clearly. Just the other Sunday, the team was part of a Sunday evening service at 'Jesus is the Answer' Church, a small church in the centre of Iloilo City. The team shared testimonies, songs, drama, and I preached. Given the opportunity to become Christians, ten people responded.

We've been flexing our muscles, too! A whole community has been relocated recently after its homes were demolished by the owners of the land. A family asked us for help. The Going Global team went to the relocation site, a long distance from the city, to see the situation. People were rebuilding their houses everywhere. In comparison to what surrounded them, this family had nothing, so the team decided to help build a house for them. There was also no water source so we have decided to dig a well for the whole community to use.

Just the other day, we went to hold a service in one of the shanty towns where a new Signpost house has been built for an elderly couple whose previous house was extremely small and unsafe. The team held a dedication service and many people from the surrounding houses gathered to see what was happening. We sang worship songs, prayed for the couple living there and listened to their testimony when later they became Christians. Then one of the team members, James Hooper, preached a short gospel talk and people, children and adults responded to the invitation to become Christians. Then we gave out drinks and biscuits for everyone there and had such an amazing time.

The team has settled in really well and we are having a fantastic time, getting used to the climate, encountering a different culture, meeting people, and seeing God use them so much in just the first week. All the Filipinos have been really welcoming and friendly. In a country where there is so much need, God is meeting and providing for his people daily. What an exciting and adventurous life when God is using those he has chosen in such great ways!

Sarah, 18
now an EDEN schools worker

Most Sunday afternoons, Steve and Paul used to come and knock on our door at Ardwick Green. When we started the *Xcelerate* course in August 2001, they'd been homeless six weeks and were both addicted to alcohol and drugs. They knew one thing for sure; they didn't want to end up in the hostel. About two hundred men live there, and the story is that the owner takes their benefits book from them all at the beginning of the week. He runs a bar down in the cellar, where he gives residents a tab up to the value of their benefits for the week. Owing to their addiction, their whole income ends up blown on booze, and they can't do a thing about it. We encouraged Paul & Steve to sign up and become Big Issue sellers, saying we'd buy copies. They used to come round and sit on our front drive, sipping a brew and eating a cheese toastie. They'd talk to us about their families and their past – but their favourite subject was God!

Glory! On Wednesdays, Steve and Paul would go to Life Challenge, a drop-in centre for the homeless. Two *Xcelerate* course members helped out there, and they also had many fantastic God chats. Many a time, they felt they were very close to leading Steve and Paul to the Lord, but there was something holding them back. They wanted to sort out their problems first on their own; they couldn't see how God would be able or want to help them. My course members had the privilege of praying with them every week. Paul and Steve completely recognised something different in us and knew it was God; they'd seen things improving in their lives since we'd been praying with and for them. The course was drawing to an end. On my last Sunday at church, Paul turned up and sat with us, and after the service, we went for coffee. He'd really enjoyed the service and started telling me about God's goodness to him over the last few weeks. He reminded me of a time when we had prayed for warmth for him, and the next day, he'd found a hat. He completely recognised it was from God and gave thanks to him for it. He went on to tell me that he and Steve had been offered a house and told me they'd be moving into it in about three weeks' time, again giving thanks to God in recognition that it was his provision.

Overwhelmed by excitement, I asked him if he wanted to start afresh and give his life to God. He was in awe that he could do this. I told him what we were going to do. My course mate Jez, by now Paul's close friend, prayed for him, then straight after that, Paul launched into a prayer of repentance, really genuine. He then ran off with excitement to tell Steve! Cool!

It took five months, but our faithful God blessed us in allowing us to see this fruit. We now have to trust God that Paul will continue to walk with him but I'm really pleased that God used me in this exciting part of Paul's life.

Nick, 23
now serving on an EDEN team

In February 2001, I felt God was calling me to Manchester. At first, I was a bit worried and felt I wasn't good enough to carry out God's work. I had been a Christian for five years but hadn't really grabbed God's love. I had a really good job but I knew it was God's will for me to give up the job, the nice car that went with it, plus my flat and move lock, stock and two smoking barrels to Manchester!

During my time on *Xcelerate* God did some amazing things. There were times when I was faced with situations I couldn't handle. I found that to God, the impossible is just not a problem and because of this, I felt the need to worship and praise God every second of the day. In these times, God gave me a passion and a patience for all the kids I was working with. My heart was softened with their despair and I really wanted to share with them God's love for them.

I've now moved on to the Wythenshawe EDEN project and every day, I chat with kids and give them hope through my love and God's love. I've found that when you sacrifice things to do God's work, he rewards you with stuff so much better than you had before.

Hannah, 25
now pioneering youth outreach in Barrow

Xcelerate wasn't just an experience. It was a wake-up call – but not just like my dad calling me for breakfast. It was louder and more frequent. Most conversations I had, most of the speakers I heard and most of the placements I went on challenged what I thought I knew. That was eight months ago and God is still challenging me – we need to realise he isn't some cartoon character in a weekly magazine. He deserves more of our territory, trust and talk-time.

   Xcelerate wasn't just five months of my life – it's the rest of my life.

*chapter
thirteen*

Xcelerate, the course

A dynamic training school which will accelerate young evangelists in their knowledge, skills, character and motivation.

'It's my pleasure to introduce to you – Xcelerate. For ages, we've dreamed of The Message including a training facility where our vision, passion and values can be passed on to a new generation. Xcelerate is just that – an environment in which you'll grow in your love for the church and your heart to reach the lost. That's a new fusion that we all need to see happen.'
Andy Hawthorne, Director

'We've established a training programme to accelerate young evangelists in every area of life, coming from the point of view that an evangelist is about who you are, more than what you do. Xcelerate contains all the basic elements of discipleship including local church life, varied experience of mission, prayer, worship, pastoral care and of course, solid Bible teaching. We feel we've created something fresh, creative and relevant for the twenty-first century.'
Matt Wilson, Course Leader

Here are our basic aims…

1. To identify gifted young evangelists, no matter how raw
2. To guide them through a course, developing knowledge, skills, character and motivation
3. To release them into a lifetime of effective ministry in the power of the Holy Spirit

Here's how we achieve them…

1. We network, advertise, interview and generally 'get the word out' throughout the Christian community.
2. We deliver a Bible-based syllabus, complemented by 'hands on' experience and pastoral care, with constant encouragement of personal vision and discipline.
3. We prepare for the future together, assisting in any future connecting process.

Where is the course held?

We've got leases on two big, comfy residential properties in Manchester, where our trainees live in the community for their time with us. We teach in a funky seminar facility in the University district of the city.

When does it start?

2002:B starts in August 2002 and runs till Christmas.
2003:A will start on the first Monday in February.
That's the pattern. There will be two courses a year; you can apply any time, even if you aren't ready to come just yet.

Who are we taking on?

The typical trainee will be aged 18-25 (ish!), with no prior training required. We like teachable people with servant hearts and evidence of evangelistic gifting. The first step is to apply, then come for an interview.

What about money?

Xcelerate is carefully administered by *The Message* to make it as accessible as possible. Course fees for 2003 are £1700, which includes self-catering accommodation. Fees must come to us before you start the course. Each trainee should also be looking to raise ongoing support of £30 - £40 per week to pay for groceries, transport and generally enjoying life in the city. We have a small Bursary Fund to help needy students and to assist with certain practical and social aspects of the course. Local churches involved in our work contribute to this, and we welcome donations from other individuals with a vision for what we're doing.

How will trainees be involved in Church Life?

Xcelerate trainees are hosted in ones and twos by inner city Manchester churches for the duration of the course. The idea is that they simply join the church family. The course leaders regularly review integration, involvement and progress with the church leaders. Areas of church life open to trainees could be any or all of the following ...

- Cell / home groups
- Sunday mornings
- Youth groups and activities
- Worship team

Prayer Points

- That the trainees receive all the provision and inspiration they need as they come to Manchester.
- Wisdom and anointing for the staff, particularly Steve and Colette who take care of the day-to-day running of the course and responsibility for the care and development of the raw recruits.
- Placements are very challenging by design, so pray for good relationships between staff, trainees and those we reach out to together.
- We're looking for prayer partners who will commit themselves to pray regularly for the trainees as they serve God on the frontline in our city.

The Accommodation:

Much of the life and fun of *Xcelerate* revolves around community life in our two houses, which are both in easy reach of the training facility.

They're fully furnished to a high standard and we've found everyone feels at home really quickly. Rooms are usually shared, which we've found just adds to the quality of the friendships made. All appliances are supplied so all you'll be expected to do is keep the houses in a godly order, which is all part of the character building. Houses are alarmed and all bills except the phone bill are paid by us.

Course Content:

The curriculum is a blend of Bible teaching in the mornings and practical opportunities in the afternoon/evening. We cover a range of sixty important topics, grouped together under weekly subject headlines. The learning atmosphere is relaxed and creative with plenty of opportunity for God to take over.

Reading Programme:
Week 1-10: The Gospels – The character of Jesus, being a disciple
Week 11-20: The Acts – The work of the Holy Spirit, the purpose of the church

Typical Week:
Monday – Friday will include teaching in the mornings and practical/pastoral activities in the afternoons. Weekends will combine church life, free time, and opportunities to serve on local initiatives. The timetable is made up of folio units, which we organise under various headlines as follows…

IN HOUSE:
Teaching by The Message team, i.e. Andy Hawthorne, EDEN leaders, The Tribe
THE BIG PICTURE :
Quality Bible teaching by nationally and internationally recognised ministries
XLR8:
Teaching by course leaders, a little bit of theology, psychology and sociology!
CITYSCAPE:
Issue-based teaching by quality Christian leaders from across Manchester
BACKTRACK:
Opportunity for feedback on things covered during the week

FOLIO:
Time spent building up a personal course folio of notes
1-2-1:
Pastoral sessions, (minimum half an hour per week)
FRONTLINE:
Hands-on serving with The Message, plus varied local ministries and the host church, 16-20 hours per week, broken down into afternoon and evening slots.

Guest Ministries:
Teaching is provided by our full time team and evangelists and leaders from lots of different networks, mainstream and newly emerging. Here's a few you might have heard of.
Andrew Belfield *(Message 2000)*, Mike Breen *(New Wine)*, John Burns and Janet Whitehead *(Youth for Christ)*, Paul Gibbs *(The PAIS project)*, Pete Gilbert and Ness Wilson *(Pioneer)*, Gordon and Rachel Hickson *(Heartcry)*, Lee Jackson *(Tribal Expression)*, Billy Kennedy *(Sublime)*, Mark Ritchie *(Flamethrowers)*, John Robinson *(EDEN Bus Ministry)*, Dave Sharples *(Frontline)*, Phil Wall *(Salvation Army)*

Practical Opportunities:
We've lined up a whole load of nitty-gritty placements. It's not all glitz and glamour – it's a realistic taste of twenty-first century evangelistic ministry.
Two *EDEN* buses, all the *EDEN* projects, Salford *LifeCentre*, *Life Challenge* (drop in for addicts), *The Mustard Tree* (soup run for the homeless), *Planet Life*,

Prison Ministry, Schools Teams, Sports
Teams, Student Action work... the works!
PLUS: at least one week-long mission
during every course.

Certification:
Everyone who completes the course will
receive *The Message* Certificate in
Evangelism.
At the end of each course, there will be a
commissioning ceremony with awards.

You can request an info pack and
application form by emailing:
xcelerate@message.org.uk

If you're interested in joining an *EDEN* team
take a look at our ministry website
www.message.org.uk and click on *EDEN*

The Message Trust is a company limited by
guarantee, registered in England & Wales,
no. 3961183. Registered charity no. 1081467

Other Products

Mad for Jesus by Andy Hawthorne £6.99
Far more than a fan book, *Mad for Jesus* reveals the dramatic stories of band members including Cameron Dante. There's the powerful account of the EDEN project, with personal accounts of the lives of radical young Christians. You'll read the inside stories of outreach initiatives in some of the toughest urban areas, plus the lessons learned along the way.

Take Back the Beat by *The Tribe* £15.00
Re-formed and re-named: *The Tribe* are stronger than ever with their latest album upping the rap/dance music stakes. Chokkablok with pumping anthems and fresh-from-the-street sounds, this striking album was the basis of the massively successful *Take Back the Beat* tour of the UK.

www.messagetrading.co.uk